FEEDING DEMONS

FEEDING DEMONS

PERRY STONE, JR.

Fedd Books
P.O. Box 341973
Austin, TX 78734
www.thefeddagency.com

Published in association with The Fedd Agency, Inc., a literary agency.

Unless otherwise noted, all scripture quotations are from the KJV, King James Version.

Scripture taken from the New King James Version®. Copyright © 1982 by Thomas Nelson. Used by permission. All rights reserved.

ISBN: 978-1-943217-86-1
eISBN: 978-1-943217-87-8

Printed in the United States of America
First Edition 15 14 13 10 09 / 10 9 8 7 6 5 4 3 2

TABLE OF CONTENTS

INTRODUCTION

I stood on my twelfth-floor hotel balcony, catching a spectacular view as the glow of the morning sunrise reflected like glistening orange-colored diamonds on the surface of the biblical lake, where *demons and deity collided* nearly two thousand years ago. As light swallowed the darkness, appearing in my view, on the other side of the eight-mile-wide blue waters was a large mountain, sloping with deep canyons into the water, where Jesus encountered more demon spirits than at any other location combined during His forty-two months of public ministry. Closing my eyes, my mental time machine journeyed back to the Roman time, as I visualized public mass confusion, after a herd of squealing swine made their last stampede on earth, running violently down the cliffs, drowning themselves in the blue waters of the Sea of Galilee. It was at this moment I realized, Jesus encountered more demons around this lake than at any other location in Israel. The gnawing question of "Why?" soon gripped my mind. It was in this setting, during a November Holy Land Tour, that much of this book was written.

The four Gospels record Christ's deliverance and healing ministry, 70 percent of which occurred in the Galilee. As stated, Christ encountered more people *controlled by evil spirits, supernatural entities that theologians identify as demons* in the Galilee region than at any other location during His public ministry. Some suggest it is because He spent more time in this mountainous section of Israel. While this is true, there was also more spirit activity, or demonic influence, in these mountains—and for a good reason. Consider the following New Testament examples of demonic encounters requiring Christ's delivering power in the Lower Galilee:

- Mark 1—A demon-possessed man in a Capernaum synagogue
- Mark 5—A man with at least two thousand demons, living among tombs across the lake from Capernaum
- Mark 9—In a Galilean city a young boy was having dangerous seizures caused by a spirit
- Luke 13—The woman with a spirit of infirmity—believed to be attending a Galilean synagogue

It appears that demonic spirits were *comfortable* in this region of the Promised Land (note Mark 5:1-14). After years of gleaning insight concerning the Galilee, the area was identified by Isaiah as the "Galilee of the nations" by the sea (Isa. 9:1) consisting of a mixed population. The citizens were often rude, superstitious, and ignorant of the Torah and the prophets of Scripture. Isaiah predicted those living in this region were in "darkness" and would "see a great light" (Isa. 9:2). Also, the Sea of Galilee is not far from the border of Syria and Lebanon, nations whose Gentile population historically worshipped idols and false gods. Wherever idolatry is strong, the doors for evil and unclean spirits to be at ease and functioning among the population are blasted wide open. This is perhaps why one man could be possessed by a "legion" of evil spirits that violently drove him away from his family into a graveyard, where he screamed out in mental torment while lying around naked, seizing citizens in nearby communities with fear (Mark 5:1-14).

There was a necessity of Christ arising "a great while before day" in intense prayer, on a high mountain prior to ministering to those in this region (Mark 1:35-45). It is also noted that the Lower Galilee (the Sea of Galilee region) was the heart of Christ's deliverance ministry, as the population was large, the land was a crossroads to surrounding nations, and the needs were great. It was in these places the Holy Spirit explained to me the new level of end-time spiritual warfare, including a powerful revelation related to the spirit world, and how Satanic battles against us are mapped out in *private* but executed in *public.*

This book is not intended to glorify the presence, power, or plots of the adversary, but is written to expose their strategies and enlighten believers, teaching them to enforce their authority, provided through the redemptive covenant of Christ! From my teen years to the present,

I have encountered the powers of darkness and have learned much regarding their operational skills, deceptive tactics, and crafty methods of battle. Thus, this book could be called "a spiritual warfare strategy from one soldier to another."

In Covenant until the End,
Perry Stone, Jr.

1 | Identifying Satan's Chain of Command

Picture with me two men, both six feet tall, both with wavy dark hair, both with a strong, well-defined physique. Both men are in the United States Marines, and in civilian clothes; no casual citizen would mark them as being linked with the military. Their only distinguishing physical feature is that one is younger and the other older.

Travel now to the Marine Base in Camp La June. Both men are now fully dressed in the Marine Corps Blue Dress. It is now quite obvious, by the insignia on their uniforms, that the younger man is a private first class and the older gentleman is a brigadier general. Physically, there's not a significant difference other than age. However, once in uniform, the younger understands the authority the brigadier general holds over him and will always address him as "Sir," recognizing both his *position* and *authority* with a salute.

Here is the question: Who or what gives the brigadier general authority to command and demand over the lower-level soldier? It is his age? Is it his years of service spent in the Marine Corps? Is it the uniform that bears numerous metals and insignias on his sleeves or chest? Or, is it his years of experience and knowledge, of military strategies and warfare? The answer is a combination of all the above. By biblical definition, this type of *authority* is identified with the Greek word *exousia*, which carries the meaning of a special ability or privilege, interpreted as "delegated influence and authority." Christ walked and ministered in *exousia* (authority KJV—Matt. 7:29). On one occasion a Roman soldier, a Centurion (a position that commanded one hundred Roman soldiers under his authority) came to Christ on behalf of his sick servant. The Scripture records he understood the power of words and how words release authority. He told Christ to "speak the word only" and his servant would be healed (Matt. 8:8). The suffering servant was many miles away and it was impossible for the servant to audibly hear Christ say, "Be healed." However, this Roman soldier understood that when Christ spoke in *one location*, the Almighty, in heaven, carried Christ's spoken words to their *assigned location*, and since God always heard Christ pray, the power of a spoken word was all that was necessary to cure his servant (see Matt. 8: 5-10). Distance made no difference.

ANGELIC AUTHORITY

Just as soldiers in the military have a specific "chain of command," the spirit world—both the Kingdom of God and of Satan—have levels and layers of authority and precise positions, indicating a higher or lesser rank of authority. God has two high-ranking angels referred to in

Scripture: Michael, called "the archangel" (Jude 9), and Gabriel. The angel Michael is a warring prince, directing his own army of angels under his personal command (Rev. 12:7). Michael is assigned as the heavenly guardian protector over the nation of Israel (Dan. 12:1) and the lone angel that deals directly with Satan.

Gabriel, on the other hand, appears in the both Testaments as God's personal messenger, carrying detailed information including the revealing of prophetic and future events of individuals and empires (Dan. 8:16; 9:21; Luke 1:19, 26). During cosmic warfare, Michael has a higher level of authority when dealing with Satan or the stronger prince spirits under Satan's command (Eph. 6:12). The prophet Daniel was in Babylon fasting for three weeks, seeking understanding to a difficult prophetic dream. Gabriel was sent on the first day of Daniel's fast to bring the prophet understanding. However, God's angelic messenger was restrained for twenty-one days. After three weeks of delay, God commissioned His angelic war prince Michael to restrain the hindering spirit that was restraining Gabriel, a demonic entity identified as "the prince of the kingdom of Persia." Binding this stronghold spirit released Gabriel to appear before Daniel with a marvelous revelation concerning Israel's future, from the time of Babylon until the defeat of the Antichrist (see Dan. 10-12). Christ reveled the varied strength of spirits when He taught that some spirits were more wicked than others (Luke 11:26). Just as some spirits are more wicked and stronger than others, angels are ranked by their levels of assignments

13

and authority given to them by the God Himself.

THE FOUR-FOLD CHAIN
OF COMMAND

In the New Testament, Paul provides his reader a four-fold order, or chain of command, in the Kingdom of Satan. We read:

"For we wrestle not against flesh and blood, but against principalities, against powers, against the rulers of the darkness of this world, against spiritual wickedness in high places."
—Ephesians 6:12

In this verse, the Greek word for "wrestle" is *pale*, and was a type of wrestling in which two opponents wrestled face to face with the intent of one pinning the other to the floor, holding him down with his hands upon his neck in a "chokehold." The loser lost more than the match, as later his eyes were gouged out; he remained blind the rest of his life. Spiritual blindness is the outcome of a person who remains in spiritual darkness as the victim cannot discern truth, right from wrong, and is void of understanding.

Among the top four demonic agents, the *principality* holds the highest rank. The Greek word for "principalities" is *arche*, meaning "first ones" or "leaders." These spirits wield the highest level of authority and are directly under Satan's command. Principalities are the unseen spirits that dominate visible world governments, through controlling the minds of leaders to pass laws (such as laws against praying in public—Dan. 6) or designing laws to prevent the Gospel message from reaching the nation. There are entire nations closed to the preaching of the Gospel: China, North Vietnam, the Arabian Gulf States, and so forth.

The next level of agents are "powers," the Greek word here being *exousia,* translated as "authorities." While opinions differ, these are the spirits working in more localized regions, and were the types of spirits Christ encountered throughout His ministry. These would include "foul spirits" and "unclean spirits" (Mark 9:25; Matt. 10:1). The words *foul* and *unclean* are the same Greek word, *akathartos,* indicating they are morally unclean and inspire lewd and immoral actions. The "rulers of the darkness of this world" are spirits that prey on not just physical darkness but the mental darkness in the minds of humanity. Darkness is the absence of light, and when the Gospel is preached darkness is expelled. These rulers of darkness are the spirits in nations that attempt to maintain strongholds on individuals who exercise some type of authority, to hinder in any manner the presentation of the Gospel.

There are also "wicked spirits in heavenly places." The Greek word for "wicked" is *poneros,* from which we derive the modern word *pornography.* The word *poneros* is used seventy-eight times in the New Testament. In Greek literature in the days of Hesiod, the word could refer to a power that overcame a person seducing them to do evil. In Greek literature, thoughts, the human heart, and the eye can all be *poneros,* or under the influence of an evil spirit. Depending upon the context of the Scripture, *poneros* is always a negative word with a negative connotation; sorrowful, unhappy, laden with care, bad, worthless, but in many instances it alludes to something morally reprehensible.

In Ephesians 6:16, the "fiery darts" targeting the righteous that are shot from one or several of these spiritual agents are called the "fiery darts of the wicked"—the word *wicked* being *poneros*. In this sense the "wicked" are not just evil people, but refers back to the four demonic agents under Satan's command, and to Satan himself, who is called "the wicked one" (1 John 2:13; 2:14).

Those who are involved in a local church setting working in their community may never encounter a high-level prince spirit, but often deal with personal problems people bring upon themselves—the lack of wisdom in decisions and yielding to the works of the flesh. They occasionally encounter a person with a sour attitude, but the "cares of life, deceitfulness of riches and the lust of other things" are the three primary obstacles they encounter. When your church or ministry begins impacting the city or state in which you live, there will be new barriers and at times laws passed that will interfere with your progress. However, once a ministry or nation begins to impact the world, both the minister and the workers in the ministry may encounter strange warfare they are not familiar with.

In the early 1990s I experienced a bizarre case of depression that lingered daily for months. It actually began on a trip to Bulgaria, shortly after the fall of communism. I was with a small mission's team of about eight people, and we were staying in the city of Sophia. My room-mate was a rather seasoned missionary, Rusty Dominque, whose journey had carried him into many demonic-in-fested nations. One night, I awoke in my hotel room and standing at the foot of my bed was a horrendous-looking spirit, about six feet tall, with red glowing eyes, gnarled teeth, and long gray hair that honestly looked like strings of steel wool, similar to the old Brillo Pads that Mom used in the 1960s to clean her iron skillets. The image lasted for a few seconds and then suddenly vaporized. Weeks later, upon returning home, a spirit of depression struck me that continued for sixty days. I could not think clearly, and nothing I said or did helped me to get deliverance in the situation. I only received deliverance after I exposed what I was dealing with and had friends pray for me. I also believe my precious wife, Pam, discerned something was wrong and went to battle in the spirit, praying in private and demanding that the enemy's attack cease.

SETTING BOUNDARIES AGAINST THESE SPIRITS

For a believer it is important to set and know the boundar-ies required for your defense against Satan's assault team. Whatever your former weaknesses were before your con-version to Christ, these are the secret weapons that the adversary will attempt to capitalize on, and stir up again, at some point during your journey.

I have a close friend who was a gambler before he entered a redemption covenant with Christ. Because of his past bondage to a spirit of gambling, he cannot play a common game of pool, as before his conversion he bet money during pool games. He will not play bingo, as if he can sense that spirit of challenge and competition mixed with a desire to make money in the process. Thus, he has set up a boundary he refuses to cross, as he knows if he does he could be back in a bondage from his past.

In biblical and secular history, a boundary was very important. In Genesis 28:22, Jacob used a stone pillar to create a boundary marker. When Laban pursued his son-in-law Jacob, the two met and made a peace covenant (called a Mizpat Covenant), marking the site of their covenant with stone markers, to remind future generations of their agreement (Gen. 31:46). God set restrictions at both the Tabernacle and Temple, requiring large veils to be hung, separating the outer from the inner court and the inner court from the Holy of Holies. If a commoner attempted to pass beyond the veil, immediate judgment struck them. If a Levite made his way into the Holy of Holies, he would be struck dead as God's law only permitted the High Priest to enter this sacred room once a year (Exod. 26). Land was also separated by specific divisions. In Israel's case, the Jordan River, which flows from Dan in the north to the Dead Sea in the south, became the border of Israel's tribal division and later the border of Israel, with Moab and Edom (Josh. 1:2).

MARKS ON THE THRESHOLD

When the Hebrews repossessed their Promised Land,

God instructed the Israelites to mark the door post of their homes and even their gates with Scriptures (Deut. 6:9) The Almighty desires His people to be reminded of their covenant with Him, in their coming in and going out. The concept of marking the posts of the door may have been inspired when the Hebrews placed lamb's blood on the outside posts of their home, an act that prevented the death angel from entering the house and taking the life of their firstborn sons. The Word of God placed on the door posts could have served as a restraining force from the adversarial spirits entering the private covenant domain (the homes) of God's chosen people.

This type of protective covenant was practiced in surrounding nations, long before Moses received the Law of God. Some of the early inhabitants of the world would have known about the fall of Adam and Eve, the story of the evil serpent, the temptation, and how evil spirits already existed in the earth. For example, over 5,500 years ago in ancient Shinar (which is Iraq today), both before and after the flood, the land was a common dwelling place for multitudes, due to the rich soil and rivers flowing in the region. This same valley region is where men repopulated and settled after Noah's flood (Gen. 10:10), building cities, including the famed Tower of Babel (Gen. 11:2). Josephus wrote that Nimrod, the mighty builder of Babel, was angry at God for sending the flood; thus he strategized to build a tower so high that if God sent another flood, he could survive, living on the top where the waters would never reach him. Babel was built in defiance of God; thus

Babylon's name in the Bible is connected with rebellion, captivity, and destruction and is always marked for God's judgment (see Rev. 17 and 18).

Among the antediluvian people, protection from spirits was so important that they would at times set at the left and right entrances of their main doors gods and goddesses. Their superstition was that these stone images would protect them from bad intruder spirits. In the city of Uruk, the city dwellers worshipped a goddess named Inaana, also called the "Queen of Heaven." In their mythology she was associated with Venus and the Moon. Her followers created ring posts out of reeds over top of the two main posts of their doorways. They placed a pole that rested inside the circle on the left and right post.

The followers of Inaana called this the "Threshold god." A common example of a Threshold god was Nergal, a strange-looking winged creature with a lion's body, a man's face, and two large wings. The Sumarians believed he was a solar deity and presided over the gates of the underworld. The oddity of this god, carved from stone and placed at the entrance of important buildings, temples, and palaces, is the possible link between its description and that of a Cherub, angels assigned to guard God's Presence, which are described with a face of a *lion and a man* (see Ezek. 1:10).

In Ezekiel's vision of God on a sapphire throne, he observed a Cherub standing on the right side of God's house (the entrance—Ezek. 10:3). The Cherub then stood over the "threshold of the house," causing the area to be filled with God's brightness and glory (Ezek. 10:4). When Adam and Eve were expelled from Eden, Cherubim and a flaming sword were posted as continual watchers to prevent men and women from reentering the garden (Gen. 3:24) and eating from the Tree of Life.

Since Adam would live for 930 years, and the inhabitants of Sumaria would have known the knowledge of early creation (5,500 years ago), these pre-flood individuals may have taken the stories of the Cherub and instead of maintaining the truth of their assignments, they may have created their own deities and false gods of protection, made of wood and stone. Without doubt, early mankind practiced the importance of boundaries, and sought protection of the thresholds (entrances) of their homes from antagonizing or malicious spirits.

SPIRITS DRIVE MEN
TO UNTHINKABLE SINS

All men have an internal sin nature, and are inclined to disobedience and to actions contrary to God and often contrary to their best interests. Why are some individuals driven to activity that is totally irrational and dangerous toward others? How can a person explain a spirit-filled minister visiting a prostitute? Or a church clerk stealing thousands of dollars of God's tithe from the church, or a children's church pastor being arrested for molestation and child pornography, or a priest molesting a young boy. The motivating force for such terrible actions must be more than the fleshly draw to commit sin, but in extreme

21

cases some type of spirit becomes inner connected with a certain act of iniquity and the person's weakness feeds on what is perceived as the pleasure of the act. Such individuals are living inside a spiritual stronghold, and eventually give themselves over to the control of malicious spirits.

All believers, no matter their age or level of commitment to Christ, will at times experience those "voices in your head," whispering negative mental thoughts tempting them to activity contrary to the Word and adverse to their spiritual journey. There is what I term "weird warfare," which is mental attacks that are so odd they must be arrows shot from the bows of carious spirits. I have met godly Christians who have questioned if they have blasphemed the Holy Spirit, and there is nothing they have done in word or deed to justify this negative emotion. I have ministered to men and women who have been happily married for many years who suddenly experience strong temptation toward another member of the opposite sex. In their minds they ask, "Where in the world did this come from?" While this mental dart is rare, some have even been pulled into a same-sex attraction, having never in their lifetime experienced thoughts in that direction. Recently, I have been amazed at the numbers of individuals in the Body of Christ battling sudden anxiety and depression, accompanied by suicidal thoughts. There is also the addiction battle: with drugs, alcohol, and pornography. Whom or what is pulling them into these pits of despair?

The motivator of all evil is the kingdom of Satan and

his agents. Satan is called "the tempter" (Matt. 4:3), from the Greek word *peirazo*, meaning to "test, scrutinize, or entice." Every spirit aligned with the kingdom of Satan is a master of manipulation, having been active during six thousand years of human history, and is fully aware of how human desires sway in certain directions; the power of one mental thought becomes an action, and continuous action builds a stronghold.

THE FIRST REFERENCE
TO AN EVIL SPIRIT

The first biblical reference to an "evil spirit" is in Judges 9:23, where the Lord permitted an evil spirit to build a barrier between King Abimelech and the men from the city of Shechem. The NJKV translates "evil spirit" as a "spirit of ill will," meaning a spirit that stirs contention, strife, and confusion. When Saul became jealous of David, attempting on numerous occasions to assassinate this future King of Israel, we read that an "evil spirit from the Lord troubled him" (1 Sam. 16:14; 18:10; 19:9). This would also be a "spirit of ill will," strategizing for something bad to occur to the person it has targeted—in this case David. In reality, the kingdom of darkness targeted David as a threat, after the teenage warrior slew Goliath. A spirit of jealousy was assigned to motivate King Saul to attempt numerous assassination attempts against David. This particular spirit "troubled" Saul (1 Sam. 16:14). There are numerous Hebrew words translated as "troubled" in the KJV; however, this word is *ba'ath* and comes from a root that means "to make afraid." Saul was actually intimidated by David and afraid of David's anointing and the favor of God upon David's life. Saul was full of self-will and disobedience that the "Spirit of the Lord departed from (him) and an evil spirit from the Lord troubled him" (1 Sam. 16:14).

In the New Testament Paul reminded Timothy that God did not give him a spirit of fear (2 Tim. 1:7). There are numerous Greek words translated as "fear" in the 1611 English translation. However, the word Paul used here for fear is *deilia*, which means "intimidation." Timothy was not *possessed* by a spirit or a demon, but was being mentally intimidated by a spirit embellishing his circumstances. Persecution was breaking out, and some church leaders did not respect Timothy as a pastor of such a large organization due to his young age. The adversary was enlarging the circumstances larger than Timothy's faith could challenge.

It is interesting to note that the first references in the Bible to evil spirits are connected with fear and intimidation. This spirit was no doubt released in the Garden of Eden, as after Adam sinned he hid from God's presence among the fig trees, later admitting to God, "I heard your voice and I was afraid . . . and hid myself" (Gen. 3:10). Evil spirits desire to keep individuals out of God's presence, and often use some fear tactic as an excuse to avoid anything linked with the power and presence of God. Jesus carried a delivering anointing everywhere He traveled. When He encountered a demon-possessed man in the

Capernaum synagogue, the evil spirit cried out, "Leave us alone" (Luke 4:34). All evil, foul, or unclean spirits are fearful of being cast out and removed from the bodies in which they dwell. To them, avoiding the presence of God in any gathering guarantees they avoid being exposed and expelled.

SPIRITS IN THE NEW TESTAMENT

In the New Testament there are numerous types of spirits that Christ and the early church dealt with. We have alluded to evil spirits, which appear to be linked with fear, confusion, and intimidation. Demonic spirits attempt to control a human body or soul, or to possess the human spirit. A "foul" spirit is referenced in Mark 9:25. This spirit was the source of seizures in a young boy; when overcome by the spirit, he lost control of his body and the spirit would throw him in water or toward a burning fire, attempting to harm him. These types of spirits are energized by the idea of harming the physical body of the person they influence. The man of Gedera was "cutting himself with stones" (Mark 5:5) as the demonic forces within him were overriding his ability to resist their desire, and the tormenting confusion led him to attempt to take his own life. The Greek word for "cutting" (Mark 5:5) is *katakopto*, coming from two words meaning "to chop down" or "to mangle" something. Self-harm has an oppressive spirit behind it. We read in Matthew 10:1 of an "unclean" spirit, a spirit motivating a person to act in an impure manner. In the biblical narrative something unclean is something that defiles the soul or spirit of a person. In the Old Testament touching a dead carcass would make a person ceremonially unclean (Lev. 11:31). An unclean spirit pushes the victim toward sin, which in itself will defile a person. Luke, who was a physician, penned a narrative of a woman whose body was possessed by a spirit of "infirmity," causing her great physical weakness. Paul also warned Timothy of the power of a "seducing" spirit (1 Tim. 4:1). The seducing spirit is a spirit that causes a person to roam from truth as they are pulled into situations that lead in the end on a road of destruction.

The English word describing an evil spirit is "demon" or "demons" and is derived from the Greek word *daimonizomai*, meaning possessed by a spirit or under the control of a demon. A person would be called "demonized" if the evil spirit were living in them or "possessing" them. Demon possession is evident when the individual has lost total control of their willpower and refuses to listen to advice and stay far from the people who are righteous and anyone who could assist in them gaining freedom from their bondage. Demons alter the personality of the person to the point that it is as though another person has taken them over and they have no control over their willpower or choices.

NAMING DEMONS

Throughout church history, attempts have been made to name the various types of spirits. In the year 1589, Peter Binsfeld prepared a "classification of demons" study based upon the seven deadly sins referred to in Proverbs 6:16-19, ". . . a proud look, a lying tongue, hands that shed innocent blood, a heart that devises wicked plots, feet swift to run into mischief, a deceitful witness that utters lies and the person who sows discord among the brethren." He listed the spirit he believed was connected with each sin:

- o Lucifer—Pride
- o Satan/Amon—Wrath
- o Mammon—Greed
- o Leviathan—Envy
- o Beelzebub—Gluttony
- o Asmodeus—Lust
- o Belphegor—Sloth

The Old Testament is the foundation for biblical revelation. From a biblical perspective there are three words, all found in the Old Testament Hebrew, that are significant in the study of evil spirits. They are *sa'iyr shadim*, and *lalite.*

The reference where the word *sa'iyr* translated as "devils" is used is in Leviticus 17:7:

"And they shall no more offer their sacrifices unto devils, after whom they have gone a whoring. This shall be a statute for ever unto them throughout their generations."

The Hebrew word for "goat" in Leviticus and Numbers is *sa'iyr.* The word here translated as "devils" is the same Hebrew word, *sa'iyr*. The goat has a unique spiritual history in Israel's early history, as the goat was a sin offering alluded to fourteen times in Leviticus (ex. 10:16; 16:9-27). On the Day of Atonement there were two identical goats that were offered by the High Priest. One was burnt on the brass altar for the Lord. The second goat was called the *scapegoat*; the High Priest laid his hands upon its head, transferring the sins of Israel onto the goat, which was then immediately led into the wilderness by a priest with a rope. Eventually this goat was pushed of a cliff (Lev. 16:9-22) to prevent the sins of Israel from returning.

Perhaps the reasons the goat became a symbol of sin is because in two biblical narratives the skin of a goat was used to *deceive* a person. Jacob covered his arms in goat skin to deceive his father into thinking he was Esau (see Gen. 27). Later in life, Jacob himself received some of his own trickery when his eleven sons deceived Jacob into thinking his youngest son, Joseph, was slain by a wild animal, as Joseph's multicolored goat skin coat was covered with blood and given to Jacob as evidence that his favorite son was dead (Gen. 37:31). The two goats offered on Yom Kippur are said by Rabbinical sources to be twin goats and also represent Esau and Jacob, who were twin brothers. Since these goats were linked to sin and sin offerings, demon spirits are identified with them as demons feed off sin.

The second name for evil spirits is called the *shed* or *shade*. We find this word in Deuteronomy 32:17, translated as "devils" in our English translation.

"They sacrificed unto devils, not to God; to gods
whom they knew not, to new gods that came newly up,
whom your fathers feared not."
—Deuteronomy. 32:17

The shed or shades are demonic spirits linked with idol worship. Foreign Christian missionaries note that in any nation (such as India) where there is freedom to worship Idols, and idol temples are filled with worshippers, honoring false gods and goddesses, there is an increase in demonic activity and demon possession. Idol-loving nations also experience extreme poverty, sickness, and superstition that accompanies the worship of dead gods.

The third type of spirit, recognized in Rabbinical Judaism, is perhaps the strangest, known as *lilith*, a word perhaps from a Babylonian form called *lilute*, translated as "screech owl" in Isaiah 34:14.

"The wild beasts of the desert shall also meet with the wild beasts
of the island, and the satyr shall cry to his fellow; the screech owl
also shall rest there, and find for herself a place of rest."

In this passage we see the word *satyr*, which is the spirit linked with the concept of a goat. The word "screech owl" in this verse is the Hebrew word *lilith*. In Rabbinical Judaism, *lilith* is a spirit believed to be a female spirit that seduces men at night. In Jewish folklore, there is a tradition (although not biblical) that Adam had a first wife named Lalith, created in the Garden of Eden prior to Eve. She allegedly rebelled against Adam and sinned prior to Adam's expulsion from the Garden of Eden. Afterwards, God created Eve from Adam's rib to become his helper. Today, in Ultra-Orthodox Jewish homes, it is a custom to tie a red ribbon on an infant's wrist to prevent the *spirit of lilith* from entering the crib as she is said to be the spirit that causes crib death.

These are the three most common types of spirits noted in Rabbinical Judaism. The phrase "evil spirit" is used seven times in the Old Testament, six times in connection with King Saul. The definition of this type of spirit is one that causes or creates some form of harm, calamity, or mischief. In Saul's case the spirit motivated him to attempt to attack David. God viewed the attack as coming against His anointed one, and removed His spirit from Saul and permitted the evil spirit to seize control of Saul (1 Sam. 16:14-16).

TWO OTHER TYPES OF SPIRITS

Some of the concepts and beliefs concerning spirits and their assignments were formed in early Mesopotamian literature in the time prior to Abraham. Later, other theories were penned by early Fathers such as Augustine, and numerous other concepts began emerging in the medieval times, as the supernatural belief in angels and demons was being revived and studied by theologians. There has been a teaching going back to Saint Augustine (fifth century A.D.) concerning two types of spirits—the *Incubus* and the *Suckabus.* For thousands of years, ancient cultures have identified this spirit with the Lilith spirit, and she is described as a woman with horns and wings whose numerous sins are under her wings. The Qumran scroll is similar to the thoughts of Solomon in Proverbs 2:18-19, which identifies a dangerous seductive spirit that comes through a "strange woman." This is a description found in one of the Dead Sea scrolls, which identifies this spirit as "the seductress." The alleged goal of this spirit is to tempt men with sexual thoughts at night. The Incubus is said to attack the male gender, while the counterpart is the Succubus, a spirit that comes in a male form attacking women. The word comes from the Latin *incubo*, meaning "nightmare." This spirit allegedly uses sexual fanatics and dreams and attacks women sleeping at night.

It should be noted that while the Bible (Proverbs) warns of the power of sexual seduction, and the seducing spirits will be active in the time of the end, the idea of the Succubus and the Incubus are more medieval superstitions and theories used to describe the sexual assaults, including carnal dream or the pressure of temptation that people were experiencing at night. There is no need to attempt to discover the name of a certain spirit, other than to identify the type of struggle a person is encountering and dealing with the source, which can be the flesh, the carnal desires, or influence of an unclean spirit. There are, however, spirits that can attract people to other people.

One noted pastor, Pastor Franklin Hunt from North Carolina, who has counselled thousands of individuals in every form of sexual bondage and perversion, noted that at times when counselling men sexually involved with men and women who are sexually involved with women, as he ministers the prayers for deliverance from spirits, a woman will at times takes on a male voice and the man at times will speak in a high, female voice. In these extreme cases, these voices are the voices of spirits using the voice and vocal chords of the victims they possess. The same occurred when Jesus spoke to a possessed man in Mark 5. At first, the man fell down to worship Christ. A moment later Christ spoke to the chief spirit possessing the man (Legion) as the demon was using the man's voice to communicate with Christ (Mark 5:9).

BEWARE OF OBSESSION WITH DEMONS

One of the biggest mistakes those in "deliverance ministry" make is to become more obsessed with the demon than with the deliverance. Inexperienced ministers will attempt to gain information from a demon, dragging out a "deliverance" for hours. This is useless information as Satan and his forces are a kingdom of liars and cannot be trusted. When Jesus delivered a person, He never led in a long prayer, but demanded the spirit to depart immediately. In Matthew 8:32, Jesus said "Go" and the spirits came out. In Mark 1:25, Christ commanded, "Hold your peace and come out of him," and we read that after the unclean spirit threw the man on the ground screaming, the spirit came out (Mark 1:26). Christ rebuked a deaf and dumb spirit, commanding it to "Come out and enter no more into him." The man reacted by falling on the ground, screaming and suddenly appearing as though he were dead. When Jesus grabbed his hand the man was completely free from demonic control (Mark 9:25-27). When Paul dealt with a fortune-telling spirit, he rebuked the spirit of divination from a woman and she was delivered "the same hour" (Acts 16:18).

During the ministry of Christ and the Apostles, there was no carrying on of a long conversation with the evil spirits, and once the man of God demanded them to come out, the individual was free the same hour—within seconds.

THE DESIRE TO BE FREE

An experience in my earlier ministry taught me how important it is that the person seeking help actually desires help. In 1981 I was conducting an extended revival in Tennessee. While I was preaching, a man ran into the church to get the pastor, who immediately exited. Within minutes, the pastor came through the front door to the pulpit, informing me of a girl who was threatening to harm herself. I told him to see if she would come in and we would all pray for her. Moments later, to my shock, two men were carrying her down the aisle, like a log—one holding her by the feet and the other by her arms. She was twisting and hollering while trying to get away. I assumed it was the evil spirit resisting, knowing its departure from her body was coming.

As I began to pray, she fell to the floor on her back, squirming like a serpent. I remember placing my left arm across her face and leaning over. Suddenly she sank her teeth into my upper arm muscle, leaving a massive black bruise. I began rebuking the spirit, to no avail. She said, "Leave me alone, get away, I don't want your help." Suddenly, through the discerning of spirits, the Lord told me, "She came to distract the service. She has no desire to be free and she likes her sin and you are wasting your time." I stopped praying and said, "Look at me. I am talking you. You like sinning and don't want help." She laughed and said, "That's right. They wanted me in here and I don't want to be here." I said get up and leave now. If you want help I will pray, but you have no desire to be free."

I later learned that she was involved in a same-sex relationship and had no desire for redemption, salvation, or to be free. She was deep in sin and there had been others attempting to pray for her, but to no avail. Two spiritual principles are evident here. First, only when a person desires freedom or there is an open door to prayer is the prayer effective. Second, if the spirit would be expelled and she would go back to the lifestyle, then the spirit would return with seven other more wicked spirits, and her condition would be worse (Luke 11:25-26). Christ cured a man of sickness and told him to "go and sin no more lest a worse thing come upon you" (John 5:14). Shutting the door to willful sin will also close the door to any type of unclean spirit that has gained access.

When studying the subject of the spirit world, especially the world of the demonic and Satanic, it is important to share with you a lesson I was taught as a teenager. At age eighteen I began ministering in local churches in three states. I was very fascinated on the subject of demon spirits and spent much time learning all I could on the subject. It was during this time I experienced a very real and powerful attack from the spirit world, one that continued for six months.

It was during this time that my mentor, Rev. Floyd Lawhon, told me I was spending too much time focusing on the devil, and if I focused on him he would show up. However, if I would focus on Jesus then he would show up. His wisdom proved correct. As you discover more insight on the spirit world and remove the blinders and ignorance, always remember that Christ and His name have all authority over all the powers of the enemy!

God of His covenant with Abraham. Moses prayed and God changed His mind, sparing the rebellious nation (see Exod. 32).

Demonic spirits know that for their assignments to be enacted on earth it takes a human, living on earth, to act out their evil intentions. A good example is when the hedge was removed on Job, bands of invading nomads suddenly showed up out of nowhere, stealing Job's donkeys, camels, and sheep (see Job 1). The plan was from Satan but the problem came from people; evil robbers and thieves. In the New Testament Paul spoke of having a "thorn in the flesh," which was a "Messenger of Satan" that continually "buffeted' (harassed) him (2 Cor. 12). The evidence of Paul being harassed is recorded in the book of Acts, where Paul was stoned and left for dead, arrested and beaten, and continually harassed by city officials and religious Jewish zealots. Satan was the instigator and the people were the tools used to harass Paul. God uses His people and Satan has his minions, robed in flesh, who listen to the voice of wrong spirits.

All demons are disembodied spirits, meaning they have a spirit form but need a body in which to express their wicked or evil desires. They cannot make visible their wickedness without a human. All men and women consist of three distinct parts: a body, a soul, and a spirit (1 Thess. 5:23). The human *body* can be struck with a "spirit of infirmity" or sickness (Luke 13), and the human *mind* can be oppressed and vexed by a demon (Acts 10:38), but the ultimate goal is to possess or influence the spirit of a living person. When an evil or unclean spirit is dwelling within the spirit of a person, this is called "demonic possession." Through demonic possession the strategy of Satan's dark kingdom to steal, kill, and destroy is manifest using God's highest creation—man.

People are the real weapons of war. A loaded gun sitting on a nightstand has not turned itself on its side and miraculously tripped the safety, pointed itself to a person, and pulled its own trigger. There is no record that a demon spirit has been able to perform such a strange task. However, under demonic influence, the eyes of a murderer looks at the gun, and the hand of the person reaches for the weapon as their thumb trips the safety and their finger pulls the trigger. While murder begins in the heart, the act itself is carried out using the physical actions of the person: their eyes, hands, and fingers. Demonic entities desire to control or possess a human body in order to perform their will and purpose. There is also a difference between demonic oppression and demon possession.

An oppressed person can still maintain self-control and not lose their willpower. Many oppressed individuals continue functioning on a job and in their homes, even though they sense a continual weight of mental oppression or negative thoughts gripping their mind. In the case of full possession, however, the person may actually lose their willpower and have little or no self-control. In Luke 8, the man from Gedera was "driven into the wilderness" by the evil spirits possessing him. The word *driven* conceals the connotation of being forced into something against your will. The poor fellow was so mentally wrecked he had no power to resist the urge to head to a dry wilderness area, separated from his family and friends.

When reading the pre-fall history of Lucifer (Satan) recorded in Ezekiel 28 and Isaiah 14, there are four conclusions about the ultimate desires of Satan, and what motivated him toward a rebellion against God.

1. Satan desired a following of his own
2. Satan wanted to be worshipped like God
3. Satan desired his own "family" to control
4. Satan wanted to take men with him into eternity lost without God

First, Satan desired a following of his own, instead of the angels following God. When he rebelled against God in the heavenly temple and was immediately expelled from the third heaven to the earth, Satan gathered a following of a third of heaven's angels (Rev. 12:4). John wrote that the archangel Michael has "his angels" and Satan has "his angels" (Rev. 12:7). In Satan's deceptive thinking, he is a competitor against God, whose goal is to influence individuals to follow the world, the flesh, and him. Satan seeks to control people who do not belong to him.

Second, Satan desires to be worshipped. Isaiah wrote that Satan said he would "be like the Most High" (Isa. 14:14). At Christ's temptation Satan expressed this desire for worship when he offered Christ control of the world's kingdoms in exchange for Christ bowing and worshipping

Jesus called this spirit a "deaf and dumb spirit." The term "dumb spirit" is also found in Matthew 9:32-33. This spirit prevented the man from speaking, and when it was cast out, the man could immediately talk (Matt. 9:33). There are, however, two different words that translate as "dumb" in the English translation. The Greek word usually translated as "dumb" is *kophos*, meaning someone who is blunted in speech or unable to talk (Matt. 9:32; 12:22; 15:30; Luke 11:14). However, in the case of the young boy in Mark 9:20, the word *dumb* in Greek is *alasos*, meaning mute. Here is why the cases are different. Those with the "dumb" (on old English word) spirits were deaf, and the emphasis in their deliverance was to cure their hearing only, or in some cases "blind and dumb" in which their sight and hearing were cured. However, not all deafness may be caused by a spirit. My wife and a ministry coworker, Tammy James, both have experienced hearing issues, caused by damage to the ear bone or the nerves leading into the ears. The young lad, however, had a spirit causing convulsion, which according to Christ was a much stronger spirit. The others were "dumb," meaning something had their tongue and they could not speak. This lad had a "deaf and dumb spirit," one that controlled both his hearing and his speech, or multiple spirits and not just one. When the disciples attempted to exorcise the spirits, they failed. This is when Jesus taught that some spirits will not come out except by prayer and fasting (Mark 9:29).

Spirits tend to take upon themselves the name or names of whatever infirmity or problem they create in the person. Habitual liars are influenced by a "lying spirit" (1 Kings 22:23). Those under sexual bondage can be under the control of a "seducing spirit" (1 Tim. 4:1). Those in extreme phobias and continually in fear may be influenced by a "spirit of fear" (2 Tim. 1:7). An individual who is battling a weakness that cannot be diagnosed or detected as caused by fatigue could perhaps be attacked by a "spirit of infirmity" (Luke 13:11). The father of the epileptic child said the spirit came upon him as a child (Mark 9:21).

On fact is evident in Scripture and that is any spirit will remain secure in its stronghold within a person for a long time, until it is finally exposed and expelled. The woman bound by the spirit of infirmity suffered eighteen years without relief (Luke 13:11), until encountering Christ. The man possessed with the "legion" housed the devils in his body a "long time" (Luke 8:27). The unnamed paraplegic at the pool of Bethesda bore his infirmity a "long time," and had sought to be the first one into the healing waters, but someone always made it in first (John 5:6). The dread of any demonic spirit is to be exposed and expelled, removed from a physical body.

Every demon has a desire to possess a body. This is the primary thought in the mind of any evil, unclean, or fowl spirit, and that is "I want to possess a human being." Here are possible reasons based upon the implications found in certain biblical passages.

1. A demon can only find "rest" when it possesses

a person, as out of the body is has no rest (Luke 11:24)

2. In Luke 11:24, the Greek word for "rest" can mean recreation—thus, spirit enjoys the human body

3. Only through a human can the spirit express its own desires, especially the pleasure to sin

4. These spirits dishonor God every time they can control a human who is made in God's image (Gen. 1:27)

5. By possessing people, demons can spread spiritual darkness and evil into the world

6. A possessed human is Satan's trophy and his spoil of war

7. Satan kills, steals, and destroys (John 10:10), and the goal of demons is to harm and destroy (Mark 9:22)

8. The ultimate goal is to eternally separate the person they possess from God, keeping them in bondage

The greatest Scripture to counter all of the plans of Satan and his dark hosts is penned by John in 1 John 3:8:

"He that committeth sin is of the devil; for the devil sinneth from the beginning. For this purpose the Son of God was manifested, that he might destroy the works of the devil."

The Greek word for "destroy" here is *luo*, and it means

to "loosen, break up, and dissolve." One Greek scholar told me this word is used when two boards or pieces of material are tightly glued together, but suddenly the glue become weak and the boards separate. Being glued to the adversary indicates you have a bondage he has linked you with and you cannot loosen yourself on your own. This means that Christ has the authority to liberate any person from any stronghold of demonic influence, to the point of complete and total freedom. Christ's final words on the cross were "It is finished" (John 19:30). Not only was re- demption paid but Satan's doom had been sealed. Christ's death on the cross "spoiled principalities and power" (Col. 2:15). The Greek word for "spoiled" is *apekduein*, which in Christ's time alluded to the treatment of soldiers who had been conquered. The victor would strip the defeated army of all their weapons and armor and put them on public display (often a parade) for humiliation and mockery. Paul wrote that Christ "made a show openly" of the demonic kingdom that He defeated through the cross (Col. 2:15). This "show" is a word in Greek, *deigmatizo*, which refers to a public exhibition. It was not just the power of the blood of Christ that defeated Satan (Rev. 12:11), but Christ's resurrection sealed redemption forever.

The phrase "principalities and powers" is used by Paul with two distinct meanings. The primary meaning refers to high-ranking spirits in Satan's kingdom that con- trol governments and the leaders of those governments. Daniel encountered these in Babylon, when the "prince of the kingdom of Persia" withstood an angel of God for three weeks, hindering a prophetic revelation Danial was seeking (see Dan. 10). Paul also used the phrase "principalities and powers" when writing to Titus (3:1), instructing the church to be subject to the governmental ruling powers and magistrates, and to show good works and not resist the power in charge (to keep peace and not create a battle). Christ not only defeated the spiritual kingdom of Satan, He also is positioned to become the "King of kings and Lord of Lords" in the future, ruling with a "rod of iron" over all the kingdoms of this world (Rev. 19:15-16; 11:15).

When a person is vexed, oppressed, or possessed by any form of demonic spirit, the person will take on the mind, thinking patterns, and bondage of the type of spirit oppressing them or dwelling in them. When that same person receives Christ, repenting of their sins and asking Christ to become their savior and Lord, then they will be delivered from Satan's control, and take on a new mind—the mind of Christ. It is time to change minds!

3 | WHAT HAPPENS WHEN DEMONS GET COMFORTABLE

In Israel, there is a region of the country called the Galilee. This territory is located in northern Israel and is divided into the Upper Galilee and Lower Galilee, consisting predominantly of high, rocky terrain and green, rolling hills. The Galilee is also considered part of the Valley of Jezreel, also known as Armageddon. The most famous section of this land mass is fifty miles north to south and twenty-five miles east to west. In the biblical time the Galilee was called the "Galilee of the Gentiles" (Isa. 9:1). In the time of Israel's King Solomon, the Phoenician King Haram I of Sidon was awarded the Galilee for the nations, causing many Gentiles to settle in this region. It was in the Galilee where Christ encountered more demonic activity than in any other place. This included the possessed man in the Capernaum synagogue (Mark 1), the epileptic boy (Mark 9) the man of Gedera (Mark 5), and the woman with the infirm spirit in Luke 13, to name a few. These encounters with numerous unclean or infirm spirits gives rise to the theory that for some reason demonic spirits seemed to be "comfortable" remaining in the Galilee. When Christ encountered the wild man of Gedera, the man was under total dominion of a strong spirit called Legion accompanied by two thousand other spirits. I have questioned myself as to why there were so many demonic encounters in this area. The answers, I believe, are as follows.

First, consider the nature of the area. Jerusalem was the capital of the Jewish religion, with tens of thousands of Pharisees, scribes, doctors of the law, Levites, and priests living in or working near the sacred Temple compound. It is believed there were 480 Jewish synagogues in and around Jerusalem in Christ's time. However, anyone who was not a follower of the true God, connected with the Jewish Temple, or perceived "religious," would have little reason for traveling to Jerusalem. The Galilee, however, was different. There were hundreds of Jewish synagogues in the Galilee, yet the region also attracted a large population of non-Jews whose religions were based upon the Greek-Roman gods and goddesses. The historian Josephus mentions that there were 204 villages scattered throughout the region, each with a population no less than 15,000. This would total the population into the millions. The Greek-Roman culture, and the fact that the region was under Roman-appointed rulers in areas where temples to idol gods were permitted, attracted many Gentiles who also placed small images in their homes. *When idols are worshiped, demons get comfortable.*

The unnamed man in Mark 5 lived in an area called Gedera, and in the biblical narrative Christ was ministering in the land of the Gadarenes. The Gadarenes were the people who populated the area of Gedera, which was one of ten large cities in Christ's day called the Decapolis (meaning ten cities). Many living there had moved to the area after the conquests of Alexander the Great and had Greek lineages. The area was located about six miles southeast from the famed Sea of Galilee on the east side of the Jordan River. The fact that the town's people were raising pigs and were devastated when their herd went into rage, tumbling into the sea, indicates the strong Gentile presence dominating the area. There are many unusual biblical narratives connected with the Galilee.

THE FAKE ALTAR

When the twelve tribes of Israel marked out their tribal land grant in the days of Joshua, two and one-half tribes—Reuben, Gad, and half of Manasseh—were all provided the mountainous area known as Amon, on the east side of the Jordan River. According to the Torah, all males over twenty years of age were required to make pilgrimage to Jerusalem three times a year—at Passover, Pentecost, and Tabernacles—to commemorate three of the seven sacred festivals, reminding them of the night God had spared their firstborn sons in Egypt (Passover), the giving the of Law (Pentecost), and Israel dwelling forty years in tents in the wilderness (Tabernacles—Exod. 23:14-17). There were three tribes whose land grants connected with or near Jerusalem's temple mount: the tribe of Judah and Benjamin and even Ephraim. However, it was a long journey from the east bank of the Jordan River for the two and one-half tribes when making the three yearly pilgrimages. Imagine thousands of men making the effort to take small ferry boats back and forth across the Jordan River. After a while, this could become very tiring.

To solve their distance issue, these tribes chose to build a *massive altar* in the heart of their tribal territory (Josh. 22:10). This very large structure could be seen miles away. The problem was, God's Torah law commanded that no one ever attempt to duplicate the tabernacle's ritual instruments and sacred furniture, which included copying the brass or golden altars. After hearing about this new altar, several tribes were so infuriated, they armed themselves to go to war with the men from the tribes of Reuben, Gad, and half of Manasseh (Josh. 22:12). Joshua intervened by sending a priestly delegation to interview the tribal fathers (Josh. 22:30), who stated that the altar was not for sacrifices, but their intention was to build a *memorial* altar to teach their children the story of the tribal divisions and why their tribes were on the east and not the west side of the river Jordan (see Josh. 22:27-29).

Moving forward in history, this same region on the other side of the Jordan later became a stronghold for Gentile tribes, and the area on the eastern side of the Sea of Galilee along the Jordan River was where eventually much of the idolatry occurred and where demonic activity was centered. After Joshua's and the elder's deaths, when it came time for these eastern tribes to make their three yearly festival pilgrimages, the distance to Jerusalem required them to make the longest round-trip journey, requiring several days, one way. For some tribes (Judah and Benjamin) the men could walk it within an hour or several hours depending upon where their homes were built. Others required a day or two, and for Gad, Reuben, and half of Manasseh, living on the far edge of the tribal regions, it took up to five days to make the trip. The center of faith and the presence of God was the Tabernacle and later the Temple in Jerusalem. It took an effort for all men over twenty to set aside the time, leaving their agricultural duties and family responsibilities to encounter God's presence during the three annual festivals. Because some lived far away from the Divine Presence, eventually false religions, surrounding pagan beliefs and idols, were mixed in with worship to God, and false prophets manipulated many deceived Hebrews. The further the people strayed from the truth, the further they strayed from God's presence, and in this type of situation, *demons will get comfortable!*

Bringing this narrative into a practical application, it is easy to attend your favorite church when your driving distance on Sunday morning is less than twenty minutes, with no traffic, traveling in your gas-efficient automobile. However, when your church is one hour away, the fuel at the pump is one dollar more a gallon than last month, and the traffic at times is smothering, it becomes easy to say, "I'll just stay in my pajamas, get a cup of coffee, and watch it on the internet," which is motivated by your comfort and convenience and not by your commitment to God's house. After changing and accepting your new "opinion" of Sunday morning church, and after a few months of Internet Christianity, people eventually ignore the verse where Paul admonished believers in Hebrews 10:25 to "not forsake the assembling of yourselves together as the manner of some is, but exhorting one another; and so much more as you see the day approaching," or in my "unauthorized" translation, "The closer you get to the return of the Lord, you need to be in a good church with other believers more than ever!"

The unclean spirits scattered across the Galilee among the Gentiles were not new devils unfamiliar with their surroundings. One of the interesting features of Christ's encounter with the man from Gedera was a request the chief spirit (named Legion) addressed to Christ: "Do not send us out of the country" (Mark 5:10). There are several Greek words translated in the English translation as "country." The word here, *chora*, is translated as coasts, county, or region. The devil named Legion was concerned that he and his cohorts remain in the same territory they were now comfortable in. Since the leading spirit speaking through the man was called Legion, and a Roman legion could be up to six thousand foot soldiers, this spirit was either taking on a name indicating there were "many" with him (Mark 5:9) or, since the same Legion (being Latin, which the Romans spoke) was part of a Roman army regiment, the spirit may have chosen this name to represent the authority, strength, and influence he observed of the Roman legions who marched throughout Israel in that day. Spirits are territorial in nature and when expelled seek to return to their original abode, repossessing and retaking any lost territory or individual (see Matt. 12:43-44).

DEMONS—COMFORTABLE IN CHURCH?

Without the presence of God among His people, demonic spirits can actually become comfortable in a church! Two examples stand out in the four Gospels where Christ, in a local synagogue, confronted the spirits controlling a woman and a man, both of whom were attending the Sabbath service. The unnamed woman in Luke 13:16 was called a "Daughter of Abraham," indicating she followed the Law and the prophets and was faithful in attending synagogue on the Sabbath Day. A physical weakness had overtaken her for eighteen years. There are fifty-two weeks in a year marking fifty-two Sabbaths in a yearly cycle. If she was faithful each Sabbath, she would have attended synagogue 936 times, bearing this physical infirmity. However, during eighteen years, 216 months, 936 weeks, or 6,552 days, not one rabbi, Levite, or priest ministered healing to her! The Pharisees were so connected to the letter of the law, they seemed to have ignored God's healing covenant promise in Torah, "I am the Lord that healeth thee" (Exod. 15:26), as they were consumed with arguing doctrine instead of practicing the Word. With the large number of sick, infirmed, and oppressed, the religious law keepers were so obsessed with following the dos and do-nots of the law, they failed to pray and meet the needs of the people. The second observation is the Pharisees had a burning animosity toward all Gentiles and according to their rabbinical traditions were to have no contact with Gentiles. Many of the miracles occurring in the Galilee were reported among Gentiles, and not just Jews, as Gentiles were more receptive to Christ's ministry, thus causing a theological rift among the devout Pharisee sect. Jesus expelled the "spirit of infirmity" from the woman and she was instantly cured.

The second narrative is the demon tormenting the man in the synagogue, who suddenly began screaming out while Christ was teaching, demanding for Christ to "Leave us alone" (Mark 1:24). The spirit did not say, "Leave me alone," "me" being singular or just one spirit, but leave "us" alone, "us" being plural, meaning more than one spirit possessed the man. Jesus would always address the primary, or strongest, controlling spirit speaking through the person, identifying the one exercising the most control. Once this spiritual "strongman" was expelled (Matt. 12:29), all other lesser-level spirits had no authority to resist and remain in their victim, and followed their leader out of the body and out of the door to the dry places (Luke 11:24).

DRY CHURCH AND COMFORTABLE SPIRITS

There is a difference between reverence and deadness. Reverence is an attitude of the heart that gives respect and honor to God by your words and actions. There are times to be still and reverent in God's presence, listening and not speaking. However, what is passed off as "reverence" in some churches is nothing more than a cover word to hide their "deadness." When believers sit in a congregation and never worship, pray, or financially give, then their belief is in their head and not their heart; in their mind only and not their spirit. True worshippers must worship God in "spirit" and in truth (John 4:24).

Years ago, a young girl who was heavily involved in witchcraft was converted to Christ in an extended eleven-week revival in a full Gospel-on-fire church. Her boyfriend was the warlock in the region. When she confessed her new faith, he told her, "If you want to go to church, then I will go with you but not that church. Go with me to the First Church downtown, because the church where that revival is will confuse you!" I later learned that the "First Church" was the driest and least "spiritual" group in the entire town, and many of the people were Christian in name only. Thus, this warlock was comfortable among the spiritually dead but uncomfortable among the spiritually alive!

Christ taught that unclean spirits "walk through dry places" (Luke 11:24). The words *dry places* in Greek literally refer to a place with no water. Using water as a metaphor for the Holy Spirit (see John 7:38), spirits will temporarily walk through waterless, dry places. Perhaps this is why in the synagogue there was a man with an unclean spirit. A synagogue was a place not for worship (that was the Temple's purpose) but for ritual prayers and study. This man and his spirit were comfortable with the routine, as no one ever taught deliverance or God's healing power among the formal prayers each Sabbath. This is also how a woman with an infirm spirit for eighteen years could attend synagogue and never receive prayer or healing.

Today, with the extreme seeker-sensitive movement, my greatest concern is that in an attempt to please people we are compromising the power of God's presence that is required for a total deliverance from sin, sickness, and demonic oppression and possession. When a demon spirit is at peace in church, then it is time to search and discover what has happened to the presence of God and the power of the Holy Spirit.

In the case of multiple demons possessing one person, there is often one dominant spirit that directs others, becoming the "leader of the pack" and the "spokesperson." At times it is easy to see when a person is under demonic control, when they express violent reactions to others, or attempt to continually harm themselves. Bizarre personality changes and bouts of deep depression are not always but in come cases can be a signal of demonic activity. At other times, it is difficult to know if a person is struggling with a DNA personality trait or some lower-level spirit as spirits have the deceptive ability to "lay low" when they choose, or to "rouse up" when agitated.

SEXUAL ATTRACTIONS AND SPIRITS

Today's liberal social culture has now overshadowed attendees of churches and long-term members. This is seen in the provocative manner young people dress, the music they hear, the R-rated movies they attend, and the free manner in which they carry on conversations about things that should only be said between a husband and wife in private. All spirits in Satan's kingdom feed off the sins of the flesh and are strengthened when individuals give themselves over to continual bondages that are always feeding the fleshly desires.

The entire world is obsessed and mesmerized with sex and same-sex relationships. While the world system including the U.S. Court system identifies this as the new "legal" normal, rebuking and at times threatening anyone who considers this lifestyle wrong, God's Word gives us examples of severe judgment that follows unrestrained sexual perversion, and gives a New Testament warning of what occurs if cities or nations attempt to repeat the iniquity of Sodom and Gomorrah:

"As Sodom and Gomorrah, and the cities around them in a similar manner to these, having given themselves over to sexual immorality and gone after strange flesh, are set forth as an example, suffering the vengeance of eternal fire."
—Jude 7

A common statement is "I have a physical attraction to the same sex." Attraction, however, is a feeling or emotion that occurs in practically every person's life, throughout the day, in different forms. You purchase your house based upon particulars you like; thus, something *attracted* you to that specific house. If you can afford any type of car, why did you choose the car you are driving now? The color, the interior, the size of the motor, the brand name?

Your purchase was based on a series of "likes" that out-weighed the likes of other vehicles. People's attractions are based upon similar likes and dislikes, appearances and personalities. It is a normal affection to have a friend and confidant that you trust with information and trust in a friendship/relationship. However, with people, when humans move from attraction to expression of affection *then a person's emotions take on feelings.* When emotional attachments are connected with feelings, this is when the relationship moves to a different level.

There are *natural* and *unnatural* affection (Rom. 1:31). Natural affection is how a young boy becomes attracted to a young girl; they mature into adults and the man marries the women whom he had "fallen in love with" when he was a youth. There is nothing unnatural, abnormal, immoral, or ungodly about a man-woman, husband-wife relationship, as marriage is the first human covenant dating back to the Garden of Eden, and the New Covenant pattern that one man would marry one woman and procreate a family (see Gen. 2:21-25). The root of unnatural affections was expanding in the culture of Paul's day, as both Greeks and Romans were tolerant of various beliefs, accepting any God or, in the Romans' case, no God, and basically held an "if it feels good *to* you, then it's okay *for* you" attitude. The sexual perversions practiced today are a result of resurrecting the ghost of Sodom and are a repeat of lifestyles from ancient empires.

A question posed to me for many years is "Are men and women who are practicing the so called 'alternative lifestyle' possessed by unclean spirits?" This is a difficult question to answer, and causes controversy possibly more than any other question. It is like asking, "Since sickness came with Adam's fall, is all sickness from the devil?" Yes, sickness is a consequence of Adam's fall from grace, but the root of all sickness is not always the devil—it can be caused by your own negligence or from unclean habits (such as smoking or eating bad foods) that eventually destroy the organs of the body.

Because the Bible is so specific about sexual activity of men with men and women with women, and teaches that if the participators do not repent, God eventually gives them over to a "reprobate mind" (see Rom. 1:28), there is no doubt that some type of spirit is attracted to certain forms of sexual perversion and can eventually possess the mind and body of that person. When Paul was addressing the perversion of his day, he called men with men "vile affections" (Rom. 1:26), and how people left the natural use of their body to perform acts that were "against nature."

There are numerous men and women in the alternative lifestyle who have a friendly demeanor, are gifted and talented, work hard, and so forth. The real test, however, to the level of control a spirit has over them is their reaction when they are confronted that their lifestyle is "biblically wrong." Some I have known will listen and give their opinions, but others shift from a normal tone to screaming, yelling, cursing, and even threatening those who differ with their opinions. This sudden change from a normal conversation to threats and violence can indicate that their inner spirit is being agitated as a perverse spirit is being confronted and raises up to prevent being exposed and possibly expelled.

Violence can indicate possession. The man of Gedera was so violent that he would break chains and fetters that bound him (Mark 5:4). When the unclean spirits were cast out and entered the swine, the herd of swine didn't just gracefully roll down the mountainside; they ran "violently down a steep place" into the sea (Matt. 8:32). The violence compressed within the man was suddenly released into the wild pigs. In the days of Noah, the sexual immorality had reached a climax when the daughters of men cohabitated with the "Sons of God," creating a demigod race of giants (Gen. 6:1-4). Moses noted twice that men were violent in the days of Noah (Gen. 6:11, 13). Centuries later, the men of Sodom (Sodomites) attempted to break down Lot's door to engage in gang raping two men who had entered the city. When Lot refused to allow them into his house, they then threatened to rape Lot if he did not comply with their demand—to bring out the two male visitors into the street (Gen. 19). In another narrative a traveling priest was threatened by men in an Israeli city. To prevent being molested by these perverse men, the priest gave over his concubine to these vile corrupters of flesh, who gang raped her all night. She was found dead at the door's threshold the following morning (see Judg. 19). On another occasion the entire tribe of Benjamin had been swept into same-sex relations and rose up to fight against Israel when they attempted to battle against this strange spiritual stronghold. Benjamin was eventually reduced to the point of near extinction (Judg. 20). Thus, this spirit of perversion and sexual confusion will raise up with force and *violence* when it senses that someone with spiritual authority is threatening its stronghold of control. It is important to remember that demonic spirits desire to work *undercover* to prevent being exposed. This is accomplished by keeping their victim in the dark and preventing the light of the truth from piercing the darkness. Spiritual darkness is the greatest weapon in the Satanic kingdom and spiritual light is the most important initial breakthrough force when reaching the lost.

The deeper a person enters into any type of sin, the larger the crack in the door becomes for the adversary to enter and gain a foothold. When these types of iniquity move from a private closet to the public forum, there is a uniting of spirits in the kingdom of darkness that assist in the spread of the vices to as many as possible. One of the chief goals of Satan is to make all sin seem outdated and acceptable, which only empowers darkness and suppresses light.

NOT PREPARED FOR TAKING A STRONGHOLD

Several of America's cities have moved beyond the level of violence in Noah's day, including the wicked imaginations prior to the flood and the violent threats of Sodomites whose burning lust rages within them. Churches and ministries are now targeted by the federal government, liberal administrations, and godless leaders if they begin speaking the truth in love to expose the danger of God's judgment in light of America legalizing abominations. Before a ministry or church begins to attack these types of stronghold, they need to understand that these radical groups are heavily financed, are highly organized, and have the secular media in their corner.

In a story that I will relate (omitting the ministry's and city's names), this demonstrates the threat to not only the Word of God but to God's covenant. Years ago, a major ministry was impacting nations by training thousands of youth and sending then as fishers of men throughout the nations. Several years ago, the ministry targeted a noted, very liberal city to expose the darkness by hosting an outdoor evangelist meeting with the Gospel. A facility was rented and over 35,000 youth were expected to attend. However, when the day came, there were 10,000 Christian youth and a protest by over 200,000 from the same-sex community. After they observed the impact of the ministry upon youth, the gay leaders secretly plotted to infiltrate the ministry by sending gay youths and leaders to the ministry, posing as though they were Christians interested in missions. Over a period of time, these devious individuals did internal damage to the ministry, and slowly news began to spread—not of the secret plot, but lies were told that caused many to stop supporting the ministry. Eventually it declined. Just as with Jesus, it took an inner-circle Judas to betray him.

Believers need to understand that our future warfare

is not going to look like the spiritual struggles of the previous generation. In my father's time, the 1940s through the 1950s, Americans were patriotic, the country was postwar united, and most politicians were honest as the three main media outlets reported the news instead of today's opinion journalism. In America, over 80 percent of the adults attended church at least occasionally, and the Bible was read in public schools followed by a brief prayer. The churches' spiritual battle was dealing with the distribution of liquor (alcohol), occasional adultery in the ministry, and occasional members who would lie or cheat on the job. The battles today are with alcohol, dangerous drugs, pornography, premarital sex, same-sex lifestyle, and did I mention terrorism?

THE STRONGEST SPIRITS

After many years of ministry, and personally ministering to tens of thousands of people, I have ascertained that the strongest spirits are those who have mastered the ability to grip a person in a bondage that is connected to their feelings and emotions. Emotional links can be become so intense that if a sexual or emotional relationship is broken, a person can enter such despair that they are willing to end their life. The empty feeling of loss overrides the rationale that they can and will recover and eventually move forward.

We are often told that we should not "live by feeling" and not "trust our feelings," yet every day we act and react based upon knowledge and upon how we feel about what we have seen, heard, or felt. The spirit world—both God and Satan, angels and demons—can be felt when their presence is near. The Holy Spirit releases to believers the sense of peace, joy, and power, which connects with our emotional well-being. The kingdom of darkness, however, taps into the desire of pleasing the flesh to trigger emotions that lead to captivity and bondage. The strongest spirits are not those that whisper into the ears, shoot darts into the mind, or paint a picture of temptation; *it is the spirits that can manipulate your emotions into following your fleshly desires*. Evil spirits actually receive some type of fulfillment and enjoyment when humans act out what they are tempting them to do. They gain some sort of creepy pleasure when the thoughts are turned to actions and the actions become your stronghold.

TORMENTING THE DEMONIC SPIRIT

A statement made by the head demon to Christ, when the Lord confronted the legion, is revealing. The demon requested Christ not to "torment" him ("torment me not"—Mark 5:7). The Greek word used here for "torment" is *basanizo*, which means "to torture." The spirit was no doubt referring to their eternal punishment in the lake of fire in which they will be "tormented day and night forever" (Rev. 20:10).

In the New Testament when Christ entered a synagogue or a room, or was walking into a town, evil spirits would often shriek out, using the voice of their victims to identify Christ. As with the Mark example, they requested that Christ would not torture them "before the time" (Mark 8:29). Christ's presence released joy, peace, wholeness, and righteousness and expelled darkness from the people.

Christ is seated in heavenly places, yet the Holy Spirit releases the divine presence among gatherings of believers worldwide. Peter said the refreshing comes from the presence of the Lord (see Acts 3:19). The Greek word for "refreshing" is *anapsuxis* and refers to breathing easy again, or to recover your breath. Christ's presence in your life and special seasons of refreshing will drive away any forms of Satanic oppression, depression, and vexation that are perplexing the souls of believers. In reality, the tangible presence of Christ will torment evil spirits!

When a sinner encounters the convicting power of the Holy Spirit, there is a discomfort in the clash between following God or remaining in the "pleasure of sin" for a season (Heb. 11:25). The anointing behind the preaching should be at such a power level that anyone listening must be drawn to Christ and have a desire to be free. This will not occur in the First Church of Wilderness, or Dry Saints U.S.A. Christ's presence tormented the demons living in the man of Gedera, and the same life-changing presence is available through the Holy Spirit and will torment and drive out spirits of darkness, even today.

4 | BATTLING THE SPIRITS OF DEPRESSION AND OPPRESSION

This is one area of which I am very familiar, having struggled with depression earlier in my ministry. Luke wrote how God anointed Jesus with the Holy Spirit and power as He went about doing good and healing all who were *oppressed* of the devil (Acts 10:38). This word *oppressed* in Greek means to "exercise dominion against." The word depression means to "press down; to depress." The word *oppression* has been used to indicate an unjust or cruel abuse of authority to control people, but on a personal level the word indicates a crushing feeling or a pressing down of one's joy and peace to the point of experiencing a mental or spiritual weight that holds a person down. Both depression and oppression are more than negative emotions people experience when receiving bad news or encountering bad circumstances. Oppression can originate from demonic activity that attacks individuals in forms of sickness, disease, grief, sorrow, and numerous emotional maladies.

There are numerous causes for oppression and depression, which include but are not limited to:

1. A mental reaction caused by negative news or information
2. The result of a chemical imbalance in the brain
3. The imbedded DNA in a family with the history of such struggles
4. An attack of a demonic spirit agitating the emotions

Seldom, if ever, would a medical doctor or psychiatrist accredit the root cause of a person's mental anguish to some type of a demonic spirit that has been assigned against the thinking and emotions of a believer, unless the medical professional is a strong believer and recognizes certain demonic manifestations. Even with the evidence, the secular field would chastise a trained medical professional for suggesting prayer as the main "medicine" for that person's relief. Take a more detailed look at all four of these oppression doors.

An example of an oppressed believer is Abraham's nephew Lot. This man and his family were living in the perverse city of Sodom, where men were openly having relations with other men and both the young and old men in the city had corrupted themselves is sexual perversion. The Apostle Peter said that Lot was "vexed daily" with the filthy conversation of the wicked and what he saw "vexed his righteous soul every day" (2 Pet. 2:7). The Greek word related to being *vexed* by their conversation (literally lifestyle) is *kataponeo*, and means to "wear down" or figuratively "to harass" a person. When he saw their perversion and their deeds, he was *vexed* in his soul. This particular Greek word is *basanizo*. The root word (*basanos*) means to "go to the bottom," and the word figuratively means to "mentally torture" a person. Every day, Lot overheard filthy talking and saw unrighteous practices being promoted and accepted as the norm. These activities grieved his spirit and oppressed his mind, as Peter notes four verses later that "fleshly lust war against the soul" (1 Pet. 2:11). This is a type of oppression caused by circumstances, especially when a godly person is surrounded by iniquity.

Because the DNA in the blood was unknown in both the Old and New Testament eras, and the knowledge of numerous chemicals that are released within the body was only known to God, we cannot give a specific example from the Scripture of a person who may have been influenced by a chemical imbalance or impacted by the DNA molecules passed through the blood line. However, modern research does confirm that certain diseases and other mental and physical attributes can at times be linked with family DNA. It was 3,500 years ago when God revealed to Moses that the "Life of the flesh is in the blood" (Lev. 17:11). Blood tests reveal the blood cell count, glucose levels, cholesterol, cancer . . . In fact, any activity whether good or bad impacting the body's organs can be traced through the blood.

The Bible does narrate the process of a spirit mentally oppressing a person to the point of depression, and this example is laid out in the history of Israel's first king, Saul.

This king from the tribe of Benjamin was selected by the Lord and was set apart from his tribal brothers when he was anointed with the sacred anointing oil by the prophet Samuel (1 Sam. 9:16). From the beginning all seemed well for Saul, as he depended upon God and observed God's instructions. However, within the king's heart was a character flaw that surfaced under stress, later leading to his downfall. Saul became filled with *pride* and *jealousy*. When the king began disobeying God's instruction, God withdrew His Spirit from the king. Strangely, Saul was not as concerned with losing God's presence as he was how he was being perceived by the people. Samuel later pronounced judgment against Saul, announcing God was removing Saul's kingdom from him and his sons (1 Sam. 15:23, 28). Saul did not fall down repenting, asking for mercy and forgiveness. Instead he requested that Samuel do something to make him (Saul) look good in the eyes of the elders (1 Sam. 15:30). He was more concerned with pleasing the people than pleasing God.

Saul's shift from humility to jealousy was exposed after David and Saul returned from a battle. The Israelite women began singing, "Saul has slain his thousands but David his tens of thousands" (1 Sam. 18:7). Accrediting David with more war results than him, Saul became outraged to the point of forming a secret plot to assassinate David. We read that an "evil spirit" was released against Saul, mentally tormenting the jealous king until the day he died (1 Sam. 16:14-15; 16:16; 16:23; 18:10; 19:9). Oppression and depression do not just impact the one individual under the weight. Oppressed political leaders will in turn oppress their people, and depressed people can at times pull others into their web of depression.

OPPRESSION OVER CITIES AND NATIONS

Having traveled throughout the United States and ministered overseas, I can clearly confirm that there are certain cities and entire nations that are under the dark rule of satanic spirits. Much of the poverty and oppression in third world nations is traceable to tribes, or early ancestors that worshipped idols and focused their attention on building temples to gods that do not exist, except in their imagination. The true God, Yahweh, cannot and will not bless nations or people who trust in counterfeit idols.

It is interesting to note that in the more westernized nations, various religions are cautiously accepted or allowed, but the one religion that is persecuted globally, more than all others, is the *Christian* faith. Whether the persecution is from Islamic radicals beheading Christians in Libya, Iraq, and Syria, Hindus burning Christians alive in India, or pagan religions in Africa slaying Christians in the rural, mountainous jungles, one must ask, "Why would the Christian faith, which preaches love, peace, and prosperity for its followers, be so repulsive to other religions?"

One answer to the "why" may be the impact of Christianity on the culture and traditions of a nation. In the time of the early church, the Greek-Roman culture accepted numerous gods and goddesses, holding a stronghold of political and economic control over entire cities. The temples were the center of national pride and activity; temples dedicated to Diane, Aphrodite, Venus, Mercury, Apollo, and other lifeless idols drew massive numbers of zealous worshippers, adding income to the local economy by pilgrims purchasing small silver or wooden idols and trinkets from religious merchants, padding the bank accounts of the silversmiths, temple priests, and leading politicians.

Suddenly like an unexpected storm, Christianity began sweeping across the Roman Empire as fast as a massive hurricane, impacting everything it touched. The Apostles and Christ's disciples taught and demanded their followers worship only one God—the God of Abraham, Moses and Christ. Once a convert to Christ was baptized in water, the next step was for them to conduct a "house cleaning," destroying all idols in their possession. Luke reported that in Ephesus, the new converts united together, collected all their occult literature, lit a bonfire, and threw their occult arts into the flames, with the collection valued at fifty thousand pieces of silver. It is unknown the particular coin or type of silver used for this estimation, but the value of the books would be in the tens of thousands of dollars (see Acts 19:1-19). Peter's revival in Samaria negatively impacted the occult business, possibly causing some to close down their shops. Following the Ephesus bonfire, the economic impact of Christian conversions was evident when the leading silversmith in Ephesus, Demetrius, responsible for crafting silver shrines to the goddess Diana, initiated a protest among the craftsmen, warning them that Paul's religion would shut down their business and destroy Diana's influence throughout the Roman Empire (Acts 19:24-28). The silversmith's uprising led to Paul's arrest. One reason for such animosity and hatred of the Christian faith during the first century was their belief in serving only one God, and that all idolatry was sin and conversion required the destruction of all idols. This belief was the hole in the money bag of idol craftsmen and thousands of temples and their priests, whose shrinking income was blamed on a new god on the scene named Jesus from Nazareth. Of course, mass conversions also shook up the kingdom of darkness and the spirits lost their garrison of idols, bringing down their dominion over the masses.

Some historians believe that one of many reasons for the eventual crumbling of the Western branch of the Imperial Roman Empire, in the fourth century, was a result of the spread of Christianity. In 313 AD the edict of Milan legalized the once persecuted Christian faith, and in 380 Christianity became Rome's state religion. With the decline of emperor worship and the abandonment of hundreds of idol temples, the economic impact on the West was focused away from pagan pilgrims pouring into Rome for the games and the temples; it now focused on Christian churches, priests, and one main religion.

Principality spirits have built their walled fortresses in cities and nations where ungodly leaders often unknowingly provide these entities access by enforcing legal, political, and religious decisions that stop or limit the preaching of the Gospel. The Gospel of Christ is the world's only true "light" source to enlighten man's darkened understanding and dispel spiritual ignorance from humanity.

In my travels, I can easily discern the cities where the greatest spiritual oppression and demonic control dominates, as the sun sets. One category of spirits Paul identified was "Rulers of the darkness of this world" (Eph. 6:12). The Greek word for "ruler" is *kosmokrater*, and means a world ruler in the spirit world. The Greek word for "darkness," *skotos*, is the common word used for darkness in the New Testament and can mean "shadiness," or a spirit that hides in obscurity but is working and lurking in the shadows undetected. All spirits whether good or evil cannot be seen with the human eye. However, a true believer has an internal sensor within their spirit that acts like a metal detector that is silent while sweeping the ground, only to be set off when it hits unseen metal buried in the earth. True believers have an internal radar that can pick up on various types of spiritual activity in the atmosphere. This is what occurs to me when I travel the nation and the world.

I have ministered in thirty-eight states and in eight foreign nations. I recall years ago in the early 1990s ministering in Uganda, Africa, in a series of evangelistic meetings. My missionary coworker and I stayed in a rather nice hotel on the edge of the city. The people were very humble, sweet, and precious, but the atmosphere at the hotel, especially at night, was tense and unsettling. I had been observing a tall hotel across the hill from ours and noticed there were large buzzards circling it continually, as a few were perched on the ground as though waiting for someone to feed them. I was puzzled at the sight and that afternoon asked my driver for an explanation. He asked me if I had heard of their former dictator Idi Amin, who had once ruled Uganda and had hijacked the Israeli airlines years earlier. I replied that I had heard of him. The driver then laid out a detailed narrative of the rise and fall of Amin, and how for many years the hotel across from us was the place where hundreds of Ugandans were tortured and killed and their bodies were fed to the vultures. He stated in a somber and sad tone, "The vultures still come to the place as though anticipating that another body will be thrown on the ground that they can devour!" Thus, my discerning that something was wrong and there was no peace in the atmosphere was accurate, as the demons of hate and bloodshed had controlled the region, creating an oppressive and depressive layer of darkness.

As strange as this sounds, many of the godly, praying saints in Uganda began observing how during an outdoor gospel crusade being conducted, it was common for a massive number of vultures to sit in the trees and watch the process. There was no outward sign of agitation among them during the announcements or even with the music. However, once the preaching began, the vultures would unite in chorus of frightening, shrieking sounds that would distract everyone at the meeting. This would continue until the speaker would begin rebuking them in the name of Christ. Immediately, they would be-gin to fly away from the grounds. My driver and several ministers said, "I know Christians in the West think we are crazy, but we deal directly with strong demons here that most Americans never deal with." My driver added, "We believe that when these vultures ate the flesh of the people, many of them became demon possessed, just like the swine were in the time of Christ, and the spirits en-ter these birds and at times this is why they distract the preaching." Not being from this culture, it is difficult to comprehend the types of spirits these believers fight in their own nation. As the man noted, in the New Testa-ment on one occasion, Christ expelled a legion of demons from a tormented man, and the evil spirits left the man's body and entered into two thousand swine. The swine be-gan a violent descent into the Sea of Galilee, where they drowned. Three gospel writers—Matthew, Mark, and Luke—all relate this narrative of the man being delivered from demons and the pigs drowning. Note that all three use the same word to describe the herd of swine running off the cliff: "The herd of swine ran violently down a steep place into the sea" (Matt. 8:32; Mark 5:13; Luke 8:32). The Greek word here translated in English as "violently" is *hormao*, from the word *horme*, which can refer to a violent impulse. Many animals including elephants, lions, tigers, dogs, cats, and even some birds have a limited type of will that bring the animal kingdom under subjection to men, as mankind was given "dominion" over creation (Gen. 1:26-28). However, once these swine were under the compete influence of the same spirits that motivated the man to become violent, the swine lost any ability to control or resist what was occurring to them. Nations where the innocent have been slain or where idol worship dominates always have a stronger oppression over their nation than those regions where the Christian faith is strong.

THE ATMOSPHERE OF AMERICAN CITIES

America is called the "melting pot," a metaphor marking our uniqueness as a nation of immigrants. From the founding of America in 1776 to the Great Depression in 1929, the immigrants that traveled by ship and later by plane to become Americans were mostly from African or European nations where the Christian faith (Protestant, Catholic, or Orthodox) was their predominant religion. Over the years, it became common to allow nationals from foreign nations to receive visas to America, opening a door to citizenship. With the 1965 Immigration Act, which removed the quota system, many people from various regions across Asia came to the United States bringing with them different religious beliefs and setting up what the Scripture considers false gods and idols.

Christian converts from nations such as India explain in detail how demonic spirits are attached to idol worship. Such cultures offer numerous offerings or at times sacrifices to appease the spirit behind each god. The superstition among the followers is that the gods are angry with a person who is suffering or in poverty, and to turn the favor of a deity, an offering is required. This is a corruption of an ancient Old Covenant law where the blood sacrifice of an animal was required by Jehovah to erase the person's sins, or offerings were burnt on an altar for thanksgiving. The adversary is the master counterfeiter whose creative ability is limited to what already exists. Thus, whatever God speaks Satan counters, and what God creates the enemy counterfeits.

The tens of thousands of rural communities in America have a different "feel" than the hundreds of overpopulated cities. My traveling ministry requires me to overnight in major U.S. cities from coast to coast. For many years, of all the cities whose atmosphere disrupted my sleep pattern, the top ranked would be Tampa, Florida. I began ministering in Tampa in the late 1980s. My wife, my son (who was a year old), and I stayed in a motel off the main road leading into the southern part of the city. Each night during the entire week at exactly 12:30, my son would suddenly awaken, crying as though he were in pain. In my case, I awoke every hour and was barely able to return to sleep. My wife found it difficult to rest at night the entire time we stayed in the area. Each year for several years we returned to the area and each time found it difficult at night to sleep. I knew there was some form of rulers of darkness in control of the city.

Later after returning each year to minister, I discovered that the "Mob" had moved their headquarters out of the northern cities to Tampa, as Tampa Bay was a perfect location to bring drugs in from Mexico. The city had

also become a leading headquarters of the porn industry. While ministering in one Tampa church, I saw a man
leaving the church's administrative offices. A staff member
said, "Do you know who this man is?" After saying, "No,"
they replied, "He is the king of the pornography industry
in the region. He owns many of the strip clubs and fights
the Christian (such as our pastor) who is trying to pass
laws to close down some of his businesses." The pastor
had been challenging the man's business and he came by
to speak to him. I was standing at my resource table and
handed this man a prophetic video to watch. He looked at
me and said, "Thanks. I like to see what my enemies are
teaching!"

Just as Lot was vexed in his soul, the spiritual atmo-
spheres in nations and cities can bring either rest or rest-
lessness to believers who stay within the borders of the
regions controlled by dark spirits.

Just as the human heart has an electromagnetic field
that can be synced with another person, all spirits have
some type of energy that emanates from them or out of
them when they are present in a room or when they are
possessing a person. This spiritual energy can be detected,
and at times the physical body reacts to the energy field of
the spirit that is present. Job described a vision in the night
where he saw a visible manifestation of a spirit. He said,
"Then a spirit passed before my face; the hair of my flesh
stood up" (Job 4:15). Job continues to write that he "could
not discern the form thereof" (Job 4:16). Notice Job could
not discern the shape or appearance of this spirit but his

flesh reacted by his hair "standing up." As children we called this "getting goose bumps." These bumps can occur when your favorite football team wins a championship game, or when your companion lays a good kiss on you. I have also experienced this bumps-on-the-arm manifestation when the Divine presence of God permeates the atmosphere. On the opposite end, the same has occurred when on a few occasions I was face to face with someone possessed by an evil spirit.

FREEDOM FROM OPPRESSION

The presence of an evil spirit can torment a person, but the presence of Christ will in turn torment an evil spirit. When the man with the legion met Christ, the chief demon within him spoke and asked if Christ was there to "torment them before the time" (meaning before their final judgment). This indicated that the devil and the demons did not fully know why Christ had come to earth. These malicious spirits were made aware of their eternal doom by the prophet Isaiah and understood they would be confined eternally in the "pit" (see Isa. 14:15). Unsure of Christ's motives for casting them out, these demons in the man begged Christ not to "send them into the deep" (literally the Greek word *abussos*, meaning "the abyss," which was their eternal abode).

When Christ comes upon the scene, the oppressive spirits are expelled and people begin thinking right. When the man with the legion was freed, he was clothed and "in his right mind" (Luke 8:35). Prior this his deliverance, this tormented soul made numerous attempts to cut himself, as evil spirits seek to draw blood from a person and cause them harm.

SPIRIT FOOD

Each person is created as a tri-part being with a body, a soul, and a spirit. Each part is distinct and separate, yet make up the whole of the person. Each part also has a feeding process. The physical body is sustained and nourished through eating food, the soul is nourished by knowledge, and the spirit is strengthened by the Word of God.

I have never lost the wonder and amazement of how biblical preaching transforms the body, soul, and spirit of a person. Jesus used the metaphor of the Word of God being bread and water, two substances every living being must have to sustain life: food and water. When we think of angels, we know they are spirit beings with a spirit body, and we often never think of angels eating. However, during Israel's forty years in the wilderness manna fell from heaven for six days, providing food for the Israelites. This manna was called "angels' food," meaning a literal food that is eaten by angels (Psa. 78:25). When all believers arrive in heaven, a marriage supper is planned in which we will partake of the bread and the fruit of the vine promised by Christ, when He said He would eat and drink with us new in the kingdom (Rev. 19:9; Mark 14:25).

The description of the manna in Scripture is a clue that it was not natural food that was in the wilderness, but fell from heaven during the night and would spoil if it was stored on the Sabbath. It was round, was white in color, looked like a coriander seed, was slightly oily in texture, and could be eaten or beaten. I am uncertain when, how, and why this is identified as angels' food, or how angels eat this food.

In the realm of demonic spirits, I believe it is clear that their "food" is not some type of supernatural combination of strange food. Demonic spirits feed off their sins of the flesh and are energized and made stronger when acts of sin are committed. Displaying your mind and your fleshly appetites will restrain the influence of evil spirits and help shut doors on their spiritual authority in your life.

5 | Defeating the Spirit of Weakness

"And, behold, there was a woman which had a spirit of infirmity eighteen years, and was bowed together, and could in no wise lift up herself. And when Jesus saw her, he called her to him, and said unto her, Woman thou art loosed from thine infirmity."
—Luke 13:11-12

Years ago, I made an interesting discovery when examining the meaning of the Greek words used in the story of Jesus freeing this woman from a "spirit of infirmity" (Luke 13). Biblical word studies are important as often in an English translation, some words may conceal a deeper meaning in the Bible's original language, in this case the Koine (common) Greek in which the New Testament was written. The interesting word was *infirmity*.

The Luke narrative occurred when Christ was ministering in a local Jewish synagogue. The custom was for men to sit on the main floor and the women to sit in a balcony that was constructed within the stone facility. Christ observed a woman who was physically bent over and could not lift herself up. He called her to the front and rebuked a "spirit of infirmity." In the West, when we say a person has an "infirmity," the word can have a broad meaning. Infirmity can refer to a sickness, a disease, or in some instances a person whose legs or arms are paralyzed. When I looked up the Greek word for "infirmity" in this biblical account, I was surprised to see a broader meaning.

The word *infirmity* is found seven times in seven verses in the New Testament (Luke 13:11-12; John 5:5; Rom. 6:19; Gal. 4:3; Heb. 5:2; 7:28). In all seven references the Greek word is *astheneia*, meaning "a feebleness or weakness." The meaning goes beyond a physical infirmity and can also allude to a moral weakness. While the primary meaning is a sickness or disease of the body, infirm spirits also attack a person by creating weakness in the mind and emotions, or, in this woman's case, her body was under a thirteen-year physical assault, evident by her walking bent over, unable to stand upright. Had she been living today, doctors may have diagnosed her with a crippling disease or a spinal disorder, or tagged some long, difficult-to-pronounce medical name to identify her physical condition. Jesus detected that the root cause was a spirit of *weakness*, and He expelled (cast out) the spirit that gripped this feeble woman, bringing her instant healing.

When dealing with the subject of an attack from a spirit such as a *spirit of infirmity*, we must remember that Satan and his team will capitalize upon any common weakness (stress, fatigue, tiredness), elements common in the natural world, and hit a person at the peak of their weakest moment. For example, if you are a workaholic and spend seventy to eighty hours a week nonstop working, and after several months experience a complete physical collapse, the devil did not instigate that problem, as you may have broken a spiritual rule by not resting one day a week (called the Sabbath). I have learned that some weaknesses are a reaction of the body to stress and fatigue, which are self-inflicted and not demonic darts.

Adrenaline Fatigue

The physical body has God-created chemicals that interact with the brain, releasing a sense of pleasure, reward, and peace. A lack or imbalance of these chemicals can lead to depression, or an overabundance can cause problems for the emotions and physical body of a person. One of the body's most important glands is the adrenal gland, which produces adrenalin to the organs of the body. The adrenal glands sit on top of the kidneys and help control heart rate, blood pressure, and other vital functions.

For years my wife told me that I tend to overwork, pressing beyond my physical limits, nonstop with an intense schedule—and was operating on my adrenaline. She would say, "You're just operating on adrenaline and need to rest and slow down!" A common symptom of excessive, exhaustive, tiredness, and drain that some individuals experience (such as myself) can be a level of adrenal fatigue, resulting from the adrenal gland functioning below its necessary level. Adrenal fatigue is commonly associated with prolonged stress. Certain types of infections within the body can also trigger this type of fatigue. The fatigue cannot be relieved by a few good nights of sleeping or resting, and the problem will impact your body, soul, and spirit. It is common for those experiencing adrenal fatigue to increase their intake of caffeine products—coffee, soft drinks, and energy drinks—to give them a daily "pick-me-up." This is false energy, and eventually your body will shut down and you are left lying in bed unable to function.

When a person experiences a major surgery or a serious infection, a death of a close loved one, a major loss of some type, or numerous other stress-related incidents, the adrenal gland is designed to release adrenaline to the body's organs, such as the heart, to help cope with the stress level. Eventually, if the root cause of the stress is not dealt with, the gland will overwork and make a person susceptible to fatigue.

Two of my very close ministry friends both experienced complete adrenal fatigue. For one man, the symptoms continued for seven years, until he was miraculously restored. For the other, it was not as lengthy but it affected him emotionally and physically, becoming the root cause of a horrible series of attacks from the enemy.

Beginning in January each year, my schedule is filled with research, writing, speaking, and traveling. This process continues into November, where I host two major Israel tours, often taping as many as thirty-six Manna-fest telecasts within sixteen to eighteen days. These programs require months of research for the telecast, creation of special outlines, and a nonstop on-location travel schedule from biblical sites in northern Israel to the extreme southern part. When returning home, during the first week of December, I have accomplished about 95 percent of my assignments for that year, and having no specific pressure to study, write, or travel for several weeks, my physical body often *crashes*. During such times I have experienced days in which I could barely get out of bed, and have almost no motivation for several weeks. Each December, Gina Bean, my former secretary of fifteen years, would observe me so weak and tired that she would say, "This happens every year at the same time and you are crashing again!"

In this case, I do not believe my exhaustion was an *assignment of a spirit of weakness* attacking my body, but the natural results of continuous activity, increasing my stress level and then suddenly coming to a screeching halting. My body literally crashes, and for days I have a difficult time tapping into any motivation and even functioning normally throughout the day. This type of weakness can only be dealt with by adjusting your schedule, taking breaks, and properly resting.

While some weakness issues are physical, others are issues originating in the heart. Recent research has given us some incredible information on the "brain" that is located within the heart.

THE HEART HAS A "BRAIN"

I was raised in a minister's home and am a fourth generational minister. Having heard hundreds of messages about the *heart*, the majority of ministers have viewed the heart as an internal organ pumping life-sustaining blood throughout the body, keeping a person alive, until the red muscle stops, followed by the lifeless person being pronounced dead. For most of my ministry I have assumed that any Scripture referring to the heart was written as a metaphor or was penned to paint the imagery of a person's secret thought life. Recent research has opened up a new understanding of linking the physical heart with the thoughts and emotions of a person.

Some of the heart verses include Jeremiah 17:9: "The heart is deceitful above all things and desperately wicked, who can know it." Christ said that "out of the abundance of the heart the mouth speaks" (Matt. 12:34). He reminded his disciples that a good man brings out of the treasures of his heart good things" (Matt. 12:35). One of the strongest verses exposing the influence and issues that come from the heart is in Matthew 15:18-19:

"But those things which proceed out of the mouth come forth from the heart; and they defile the man. For out of the heart proceed evil thoughts, murders, adulteries, fornications, thefts, false witness, blasphemies."

Christ understood that the words coming from a person's *mouth* are actually coming from the *heart*. My question is how could a red muscle in a person's chest, pumping blood, have any influence over someone's conversations or thoughts? For years I taught that when we read biblical passages related to the "evil" in the heart it was referring to the human *mind*, since we all think and speak using our mental intellect. However, new medical and scientific research has proven that the heart is more than a pump organ that maintains life. Research now recognizes that the heart has its *own functioning brain*!

Neurocardiology research indicates that the heart has a center for receiving and processing information through the *heart's own nervous system*. Science once thought that the brain was the center of all signals released to the body. However, new experiments indicate that the heart can receive and process information independent of the brain's cerebral cortex. Studies indicate that signals coming from the heart to the brain actually influence higher brain centers, including the areas of perception and emotions. The heart communicates to the brain through the body via electronic field interactions. The real stunner is that the magnetic component in the heart is five thousand times stronger than the brain's magnetic field.

The heart's magnetic field caries information for the entire body. Observe when a person is in an intensive care unit. They can be hooked up to specific machines that monitor not just the heart rate but numerous other measurements that assist doctors in treating the person. Perhaps you have personally observed how your heartbeat increases immediately following sudden or dangerous changes in your surroundings or circumstances. The beat becomes faster or slower with emotions of anger, fear, stress, hate, love, faith, and peace. Mental dialogue also impacts the function of the heart. When a person engages in a conversation moving toward an argument, the heart rate increases, and some begin sweating as the breathing rate increases.

THE HEART HAS A MIND OF ITS OWN

I have often heard individuals tell others to just "trust their heart" or to "follow their heart." This sounds simple and sincere but can actually be risky and dangerous, depending upon the spiritual condition of the person's heart. For example, how many young girls "followed their hearts" when dating a young man and the relationship ended in an emotional train wreck? Or what about the husband who was married to a wonderful wife for many years, but allowed another lover into his heart, leaving his lifelong companion? Should they have "followed their heart"?

Information can also be stored within the heart. In one of the most stunning studies, doctors began to observe how patients who received another person's heart after transplant surgery began to experience drastic changes in their likes and dislikes, including the food they ate and the types of people they befriended. In some cases, the heart recipient, while sleeping, would consistently experience the same nightmare. In one major study, the researchers gleaned information on the emotional and mental changes in the new heart recipients, comparing them with the history of the person whose transplanted heart they had received. In most cases the recipient knew nothing about the person whose heart now beat in their chest, but strangely, the researchers discovered recipients often took on ideas, beliefs, likes, and dislikes of the person who had passed away and whose heart they received. One girl received the heart of a girl killed in an auto accident. The accident victim lived a few days before passing and told her mother she could feel the impacts on her head and still see the glass breaking. The heart recipient, a young girl, began having dreams of having a car accident and her head smashing through the front windshield. The female recipient knew nothing about her donor's car accident, but apparently the memory was imbedded in the "brain" of the accident victim's heart. Numerous case studies indicate that the thoughts, feelings, and ideas are somehow encoded in the human heart and when transplanted, the heart can feed the brain the very thoughts, ideas, and emotions of the former person.

HEART TO HEART ATTRACTION

The following information from the heart research study is perhaps the most intriguing and will answer a question that has puzzled believers for centuries. What causes two people to be attracted to one another, when they have never met and have never carried on a conversation? For example, there are men and women who have come out of the gay lifestyle and have told me that to this day they can walk into a business office, a sports arena, or even a local church and can within seconds sense if a person standing near them or greeting them is presently in the gay lifestyle, or if they are secretly practicing the lifestyle.

The same is true if a person has a weakness for the opposite sex. During years of ministry I have met individuals
who struggled with a spirit of adultery, or some form of
sexual immorality. After being redeemed and made whole
in Christ, some have related to me that to this day if there
is a member of the opposite sex that has the "sexual spirit" or a "seducing spirit" similar to what they previously
fought, that when they shake their hands they can sense
a seductive type of energy emitting from that person. Of
course this is a troubling experience for anyone whose
past lifestyle was a continual battle of the flesh. So what
causes these feelings or impulses to be transferred from
one person to another, or a "signal" to be picked up by
someone standing near them, similar to an antenna cap-
turing invisible radio waves that are passing through the
atmosphere?

The heart research study indicates that the nervous
system in the heart acts like an antenna that can actually
respond to the electromagnetic fields surrounding
the hearts of others. Researchers discovered that the
electromagnetic fields between two people's hearts can be
measured *at five feet apart*! Another way of putting this is
to say that one person's brain waves can scrutinize with
another person's heart. In brief, what a person is thinking
can apparently be felt in the heart of another person. This
can be both a positive and negative. First the positive.

The Scripture reveals that as believers our spirits
"beareth witness" that we are children of God (Rom.
8:16), and we bear witness with one another when we are

in the faith. The phrase "beareth witness" is to "join together or to testify with." I have walked into an airport or a restaurant not knowing anyone in the facility. I would greet someone with a "good morning" or "How are you today?" and I immediately knew they were believers in Christ. Something "clicked" within my spirit that this person knew Christ. This is only possible if the presence of Christ *within me* can sense the presence of Christ *within them*. This is the meaning of "bearing witness" with another person. Being able to sense the heart of another person, or discerning the secrets in their heart, can be considered the "discerning of spirits," one of the nine gifts of the Holy Spirit listed in 1 Corinthians 12:7-10. The word *discern* means to "separate something completely for an inspection or to properly judge it." When a believer is required to deal with unbelievers in secular matters, it is important that the believer exercises the ability to discern the secrets within the other person's heart, to prevent the believer from entering into a business agreement or a partnership that could be detrimental for the believer (1 Cor. 14:25).

The negative side of this heart magnetism is if a person easily finds themselves in a vulnerable situation when they struggle with a specific moral or spiritual weakness and can pick up on what some call the "vibes" emitting from another person who also is battling the same weakness. If you have noticed, people immediately become attracted to those things that are in their hearts, whether good or bad. Praying people attract praying people, worshipper attract worshippers, Word lovers attract Word lovers, and negative, depressed, or unhappy people band together in an emotional bond.

Many years ago, a married traveling evangelist was preparing to conduct a revival in a local church. After arriving, the pastor's wife warned the evangelist's wife that a man in the church (the sound man) had been having marital difficulty, and cautioned her to be careful working around him, knowing she would tape her husband's messages each night, using the sound equipment located near the sound board. The revival continued nightly for many weeks. The pastor's wife became troubled in her spirit when she would see the evangelist's wife sitting in the sound booth beside the sound man. The evangelist's wife "blew off" the pastor's wife's concern, reminding her all she was doing in the sound booth was overseeing the messages being taped. Each morning, however, the evangelist's wife would "disappear" and come back later in the evening, saying she was out shopping or visiting around while her husband was studying. The end of the story was she became physically involved with this sound man. The same spirit concealed in the sound man's heart acted as a magnet when it sensed the same weakness in her heart, and when the two were close to one another these two "heart magnetic fields" began to "click." However, the end result was this minister and his wife divorced. It is this heart connection that Satan will take advantage of. This is why we are to guard our heart with all diligence.

When people are in spiritual agreement and flowing

as one unit they have "one mind and one heart" (Phil. 1:27). I am blessed when I meet a pastor and discover we believe alike, think alike, and desire to experience the same spiritual result in God's Kingdom. This unity in spirit leads to lifetime friendships and bonds that I call "The brotherhood of blood!" Like David and his covenant friend Jonathan, I have my minister friend's "back" and he has mine. A pure heart will connect with a pure heart, a corrupt heart will attract a corrupt heart, and an evil heart will be drawn to an evil heart. Spirits will capitalize on the weaknesses of any individual and use their mental darts to connect with others battling the same weakness.

SPIRITS DETECT WHAT IS IN THE HEART

The fact that the heart has a brain of its own with a specific "field" that emerges from it can also help explain how *faith* and *unbelief* can be sensed in a congregation of people. In Nazareth, Christ detected spiritual unbelief (lack of faith) within His small hometown synagogue, which limited His ability to perform miracles among them (Matt. 13:53-57). On other occasions Christ could discern the faith emerging from a person and would pray a healing prayer, providing deliverance for them (Matt. 9:2).

Since these heart electromagnetic fields are literal and do exist, it can also explain how demonic spirits are keen to discern whom to target with their assaults. Jesus said, "Out of the heart proceeds . . ." The negative and positive thoughts are captured in the "brain" of the heart and relayed to the brain center of the mind. Is it possible that many thoughts originate in the heart and once relayed to the brain, images are formed on the mental screen of thoughts and imaginations, instead of the opposite where images being produced in the mind are relayed to the heart? When Jesus said that murder proceeds from the heart, then the heart is where evil thoughts begin and the image or plan of how to enact the crime is sketched out in the imagination process within the brain. Jesus taught that adultery begins in the heart. We think of adultery as being a physical sexual act between a man and woman, especially one or both who are married. However, Jesus said that if a man looks at a woman (to desire her) in his heart, he has already committed adultery. This seems like a strong statement, especially when mental temptation is not a sin, but becomes sin when it is conceived and *acted upon* (James 1:15). One scholar may have clarified this statement as he believed it could be translated to mean that if a man *continually looks upon* a woman (to gaze on her) to desire her, it will eventually lead to adultery. One fact is clear—the words of a person's mouth originate from the heart (Matt. 12:34) and the heart can control both the good and the bad emitting from a person's spirit.

I do not believe the adversary can read every thought swirling within a person's mind. However, the spirit world picks up on the energy emerging from the heart field and can intercept certain thoughts using temptation (which is mental pressure) processed by images transferred from the mind (sight) to the heart. Peter wrote of people with "eyes full of adultery" (2 Pet. 2:14), implying that the sense of sight (the eyes) are the beginning point of transferring what is captured by the heart and mind.

Any spiritual transformation must include a "new" *heart* and a "renewed" *mind*. To "repent" refers not only to saying, "I am sorry and regret my actions;" it also means "to turn around and walk in the proper direction." We have the ability to choose right and wrong with our thinking and can actually pull down negative mental strongholds. However, the heart must be transformed as God creates in us a new heart, providing a new thinking process. David understood this in Psalms 51:10 when he cried out for God to "Create in me a clean heart, and renew in me a right spirit."

Heart transformation can only be accomplished through the redemptive blood covenant provided by Christ. In the Bible the Hebrew word for "covenant" is *berith*, the root verb meaning "to cut." The Old Testament biblical covenants were always linked to shedding of blood: the blood of a sacrificial animal, the blood during the act of circumcision, and the blood of the New Covenant shed at Christ's scourging and His crucifixion.

How unique that all biblical covenants involving blood require some form of sacrifice—animals in the old covenant and Christ's blood in the new covenant. The heart is the center of the body, and without blood there is no life. The Word of God focuses on the heart and God's ability to change a person's entire character through a spiritual "heart transplant," forming a new creation in Christ Jesus

(2 Cor. 5:17).

CAPITALIZING ON THE WEAKNESS

The internal pressure forced upon a person by mental temptation often becomes the open door the adversary enters, releasing a spirit of weakness to badger and harass its victim to the point of physical, mental, and spiritual collapse. For example, after forty days of fasting, Christ was left physically weak and hungry. Satan's temptation, demanding Christ to "turn stones into bread," was not in play, until the proper moment when Christ was being overwhelmed with hunger pangs. Luke recorded, "And afterwards he hungered, and the devil said . . ." (Luke 2:2-4). Using Christ as our example, when we become physically, mentally, or spiritually weak through fasting, or through sickness, trials, and temptations, the enemy will attempt to build layers of *weakness upon weakness*. Paul understood this fact, being an Apostle was arrested, imprisoned, beaten with rods, stoned, and shipwrecked, and who had endured hard suffering, for the Gospel's sake (see 2 Cor. 11). Paul also, however, understood the *grace* and power of God available to overtake each weakness. He wrote, "And he (God) said to me, my grace is sufficient for thee: for my strength is made perfect in weakness . . ." (2 Cor. 12:9). Christ fought His moment of weakness by verbally quoting the written Word of God during each set of temptations (see Luke 4:1-13). Paul dealt with his physical abuse and harassment by leaning heavy upon the grace of God to strengthen and sustain him (2 Cor. 11:24-27).

When you depend upon the Lord, He places Satan, that "roaring lion" (1 Pet. 5:8), on a leash, limiting his reach into your life. We read that God will not allow you to be tested above what you are able to bear, but will help provide a way of escape (1 Cor. 10:13).

As an example, Job was the wealthiest man in the West (Job 1:1-3). When Satan requested to test Job's integrity, God removed His protective hedge. Job, however, survived the first round of tragedies after losing all his livestock along with ten children and their homes (Job 1:4-19). Seeing that Job's confidence in God was unshaken, Satan set a second assignment to wreck Job's health. God stepped in and said Satan could attack Job's flesh but he could not take Job's life (Job 2:1-6). Satan, the accuser and the roaring lion, was on a rampage, but God still had the lion on a leash around his neck! Satan's plan was to put infirmities on Job's body, making him curse God and give up. Neither strategy worked.

REMOVING SPIRITS OF WEAKNESS

A believer must discern the cause of their weakness. Is the physical weakness caused by improper care of the body, such as poor eating habits, lack of proper rest, or abuse through overwork? If so, don't blame that wiped-out feeling on some invading spiritual power. Are the mental weaknesses a result of overwork, staying up too and too late on social media, or viewing things on the internet that are opening doors for wild imaginations? Is your spiritual malfunction resulting from a lack of Bible reading, prayer, or fellowshipping with other believers? All of the above are self-inflicted darts that are weakening your strength in the Lord.

However, a true spirit of infirmity must be expelled though prayer and spiritual authority. In the case of the woman in the synagogue, Christ rebuked the spirit of infirmity, then laid hands upon the woman, releasing healing to her body. The woman could not in her own strength lift herself up. An infirm spirit pulls a person down and capitalizes on their weakness.

RELIEF FROM THE HOLY SPIRIT

One of the most marvelous verses in the New Testament is penned by Paul in Romans chapter 8:

> *"Likewise the Spirit also helps in our weaknesses. For we do not know what we should pray for as we ought, but the Spirit Himself makes intercession for us with groanings which cannot be uttered. Now He who searches the hearts knows what the mind of the Spirit is, because He makes intercession for the saints according to the will of God."*
> —Romans 8:26-27, NKJV

The KJV says the Spirit "helpeth." This word in Greek is *sunantilambetai,* meaning to take hold of something together with the other person. The prefix *sun* is a word meaning to connect to someone else, such as coming into an agreement or partnership. Paul spoke of not knowing "what" to pray for. The word *what* seems insignificant here, but the Greek word is *tis*, and can refer to even a *very little thing*. Paul is emphasizing that not only at times do we not know *how* to pray for big, complicated situations, but we can get stuck on how to pray for the littlest things. The Holy Spirit makes intercession for us in the big and small thing! This Greek word *helpeth*, used only here, refers to the Spirit stepping in on our behalf, with the idea of rescuing or directly helping someone out of a tough situation.

The adversary takes advantage of any physical, emotional, and mental weakness. The woman in Luke 13 was struck with a physical weakness, while the man of Gedera in Mark 5 was attacked in his spirit, mind, and emotions. Christ personally helped bring freedom to victims and countless others during His ministry. When Christ departed He left with us the "other comforter," the Holy Spirit (John 16:7). His assignments are numerous, but His man goal is to be our personal helper. It is He who anoints ministers with authority and power to pray the prayer of faith, rebuking demonic forces and bringing relief to the seeker. The Holy Spirit will take ahold of our weaknesses and strengthen us inwardly for the assignments of the kingdom. Paul said it this way:

"For which cause we faint not; but though our outward man perish,
yet the inward man is renewed day by day."
—Corinthians 4:16

6 | DEFEATING CHRONIC BATTLES AND REPETITIVE SPIRITS

"Wherefore we would have come unto you, even I Paul, once and again; but Satan hindered us."
—1 Thessalonians 2:18

"A thorn in the flesh . . . I besought the Lord three times to remove it, he said my grace . . ."
—2 Corinthians 12:8

The easiest promises to break are "self-promises," where you attempt to hold yourself accountable without any outside eyes to watch your actions or outside set of hands to pull you away from the magnetic pull of negative activity. Have you ever told yourself "I am going to stop this habit right now" and only one week later be back at the same habitual cycle? Weak Christians can become influenced by wrong people pulling them away from church and prayer. The fleshly weak believer will continually say to themselves, "I am going to break off with this person as they are pulling me down." Their *intention* to follow up and actually cut the umbilical cord is honorable, but their *willpower* is soon trampled into the dust when the person charms their way through the door and once again you are stuck in a cycle that you can't get free from. Once again, one desire overrides the other desire and the weakness wins another round in the ring of life.

There is an issue among believers Paul identified as "weights and sins" (Heb. 12:1). Bible students are aware of what God has marked in Scripture as sins, as they are clearly listed; examples of such are found throughout the Scripture. Weights, on the other hand, are the little foxes that spoil the vine, which I call "pet sins." Pet sins can be an unclean habit—something that may not "condemn you to hell" but will become a continual distraction. It is possible to be stuck in a chronic sin or weight cycle that you are finding difficult to break. *A chronic struggle feeds off of a weakness that enables the problem to recycle each time the weakness manifests.*

The word *chronic* means "something persistent, reoccurring; a repetitive cycle that occurs within a brief space of time." During my ministry I have met people who suffer from chronic illnesses; when one sickness is cured another type of affliction rises. Much of their life is spent medicating one form of physical malady or another. Chronic depression is often labeled manic depression. Millions of people suffer from depression cycles that agitate them into feeling like they are going in circles, carrying an emotional weight without any relief. I have met some individuals who are chronic complainers. They literally never have anything positive to say about anything, yet say they want help. It reminds me of what Albert Einstein said: "Insanity is doing the same think over and over again and expecting a different result!" Whether the circumstances are repetitive habits, addictions, or struggles, what does the Scripture teach about being stuck in a cycle of defeat?

THE BIBLE'S CHRONIC TROUBLE CHAPTER

Mark's Gospel chapter 5 is what I call the "chronic struggle" chapter of the Bible. This single chapter deals with three different individuals experiencing three different types of battles.

Mark 5:1-20 details an unnamed man whose demonic possession left him with a chronic mental and emotional battle being controlled by outside spiritual forces that drove him from his friends and family. In the same chapter an unnamed woman is dealing with a persistent hemorrhage and can find no relief from her suffering (Mark 5:25-34). Her battle was a physical struggle as her sickness, according to Moses' law, made her unclean and banned from being in crowds with others. The third example is a young, unnamed girl whose sickness made her a fatality. This was a physical battle that became a spiritual one and eventually an emotional one for her family, especially her father.

It is interesting that Mark noted in two of the three examples the length of time the individuals suffered. The man controlled by evil spirits was possessed a "long time" (Luke 8:28). The woman with the "issue of blood" was afflicted for twelve years (Mark 5:25). The young girl was in her home and died after an unspecified length of time. The details within the Scripture of these three chronic sufferers present parallel images of chronic struggles being experienced today.

FLOWING ISSUES

The Scripture reveals an unnamed woman had endured a chronic affliction for twelve years. We read where she "suffered" many things from physicians but was growing worse (Mark 5:26). The word *suffered* means "painful sensations." In that day medical technology was limited and many so-called cures would be considered "quack cures" today. Her struggle was with an "issue." Matthew speaks of her having an "issue of blood" and uses the Greek word *haimorrheo*, which translated as hemorrhage. Mark, on the other hand, chose a different Greek word for issue, *rhusis*, which refers to something rushing, indicating this was a serious flow that was continuous.

When we say "issues," they are those things in our lives that create conflicts. Just as this woman dealt with a flowing issue, every person has issues that flow from them. Every person must deal with their own specific issues of life, for from the heart flows the issues of life (Prov. 4:23). When the woman with an issue encountered Christ's touched, immediately the flow stopped and she was made "whole" (Matt. 9:22).

GRAVEYARD LIVING

Our second example is one of the most dramatic deliverances in the Bible. This man lived in a community in the Galilee and according to the text had friends and a home (note Mark 5:19). We are uncertain of what triggered his mental breakdown; however, something "snapped" in him and he was driven by unclean spirits into a local graveyard. In the narrative this one man was possessed by two thousand spirits. This may seem impossible until understanding that spirits possess human bodies and once a person dies and the human spirit is separated from body, the demonic spirits no longer remain in the empty shell of the physical body, but depart the dead person, looking for another human to possess.

In Christ's time when a person died, they were not embalmed, neither was a funeral held two or three days later, but the departed person was wrapped in a shroud and laid to rest in a notch that was cut into a limestone cave. If a person was possessed with evil spirits, then immediately after death the spirits would seek out another person to possess. Christ pointed out that when an unclean spirit comes out of a man, he departs but then seeks to return and will bring "seven other spirits more wicked than himself" (Luke 11:26). Because this man was already possessed and was living hiding out in the tombs (caves) where the dead were buried, then the unclean spirits would seek out another person and this man was in the region, a human vessel whose spirit was open to being controlled by demon power. Notice in Mark 5:5, he was "cutting himself with stones." Cutting is a widespread method some youth use, cutting their arms in order to bleed, as a type of release from the mental and emotional anguish overpowering them. This is actually a suicide spirit attempting to force upon the youth a premature death.

During the moment of his deliverance, two thousand wild pigs became possessed by the spirits and immediately ran violently down a cliff into the sea and were drowned. Animals do not have the same control over their will as do humans. God gave man dominion over the animal kingdom. It is apparent that the chief spirit in control of its victim was a spirit pressuring the man to take his life. The "cutting with stones" was ineffective, but the pressure to harm himself was prompted by the voices within, driving him toward self-destruction. The crying, cutting, confusion cycle ended when Christ intervened.

A Daughter Who Dies

Looking at Mark's third example, we read of Jairus' daughter. The narrative begins by this man, a ruler of a Jewish synagogue, approaching Christ to come to his house and heal his sick daughter. Because of the crowds Christ arrived "too late" and the little girl died. When entering the house, Christ told the people she was "sleeping." Immediately those in the home began mocking Christ as they knew she was dead and not sleeping. Christ demanded that the mockers be removed from the room where the corpse lay, and he shut the door behind him. My first point is, when it is time to remove chronic trouble we must get rid of chronic complainers.

This is an important spiritual principle. When you are dealing with a struggle you must separate the mockers from the believers, as the mockers inspire doubt and unbelief, which always prevents miracles (see Matt. 13:58; 17:20). In the days of Abraham, Ishmael, a son born of the flesh through Hagar, began mocking Isaac, a son born of a promise. The promise could not coexist with the mocker, and Sarah forced Abraham to separate the two (see Gen. 21).

This one girl was locked in a room alone with Jesus, and that is when new life was imparted into her. Dead things cannot survive in the presence of absolute life. A chronic, lingering sickness took her away prematurely. However, one stronger than death, a stronger than the strongman (Luke 11:21-22), entered the death chamber and exited with a living girl.

The challenge of dealing with chronic battles is a person can become so used to a chronic struggle that you never expect a breakthrough!

FACE-TO-FACE ENCOUNTER

All three of these individuals had one thing in common; they all had a face-to-face encounter with Jesus Christ. Yet in each instance the *method Christ* used was different. In the case of the possessed man, Jesus *rebuked* the devils by commanding them to "come out" of the man (Mark

5:8). When the woman received her instant healing, it was a result of a *transfer* of the healing anointing from Christ into her body. Christ felt "virtue" go from His body (Mark 5:30). In the KJV, the word *virtue* is translated from the Greek word *dunamis*, which refers to supernatural power that abides within a person. It is the same Greek word used in Acts 1:8, when Christ predicted a believer would receive "power" (*dunamis*) after the Holy Spirit came upon them. In the third miracle, when the daughter was raised from the dead, it required the spoken word, uttered under the authority of the Holy Spirit, the heavenly agent who energizes and quickens the dead (Rom. 8:11). Christ said His words are "spirit and they are life" (John 6:53); thus, His words released life into the girl.

A personal encounter with Christ can and will break chronic cycles of sin and defeat. I call the initial encounter of this type radical conversion. The word *radical* has evolved into meaning someone who is extreme and violent in expressing their opinions. The original word, however, from the Latin, referred to someone who went to the *root* or back to the origin. It was later used of a reformer who went back to the original teaching of the Bible. A radical conversion is a conversion that gets to the root of the problem. Whether it is demonic, carnal, emotional, or rooted in bad thinking, a radical conversion will break bondages and turn a person around 180 degrees. An example of a radical conversion is when a complete alcoholic is set free instantly by the power of God, through prayer and intercession. Or when a drug addict is instantly delivered and loses all desire to return to their addiction. I have a friend who once sold and took hard drugs, and the moment he accepted Christ all desire for any form of drugs departed from him. His deliverance was not some "mind over matter," or "Repeat 'I am free' 100 times a day;" he believed in his heart and confessed his freedom through Christ with his mouth, and something supernatural happened inside of his heart and spirit. God is the original heart surgeon, and can replace the cold, sinful, calloused heart with a new heart. When David sinned with Bathsheba and set up her husband to be killed, he later repented and said, "Create in me a clean heart oh God, and renew a right spirit within me" (Psa. 51:10).

At times a complete deliverance—body, soul, and spirit—may require anointed saints or ministers to "lay hands" upon a person and pray for the individual to be set free. This was a primary method used by Christ during His healing ministry (Luke 4:40). Jesus did two specific things when He met the woman who was bound by the spirit of infirmity. He discerned her case and *rebuked the spirit*, commanding it to leave, then He *laid His hands upon her* to make her whole in body.

It is important that those who minister through laying on of hands are living a pure lifestyle and have spent time in fasting and prayer. Paul in his letter to Timothy admonishes him to honor the elders who were faithful with double honor and to "Lay hands suddenly on no man" and not to be a "partaker of another man's sins" (1 Tim. 5:22). When a bishop was ordained the elders laid their hands upon them and this act placed a public approval upon them, as spiritual and moral leaders of the congregation. If a bishop was practicing sin and hands were laid upon him, it would be as though the elders were placing approval upon his sinful lifestyle. There was discretion exercised in the process.

When Christ ministered to the sick He would touch them or lay hands upon them. Notice He first rebuked the spirit in Luke 13, and afterward laid hands upon the woman. He often spoke and commanded evil spirits to depart before touching the person, as the Pharisees would begin the rumor that by Him touching the person He was in alignment with the demons.

When prayer and the laying on of hands is offered, the individual(s) praying and person receiving must both be in a faith agreement, nothing wavering. Jesus was anointed with the "Holy Spirit and with power" (Acts 10:38), which enabled Him to rebuke all sickness and spirits, bringing relief to multitudes.

Once a person has received the glorious touch of the Spirit, and the stronghold has been broken, it is important for them to begin the process of renewing of their mind, on a consistent basis. In Christ, "Old things are passed away and all things are become new" (2 Cor. 5:17). Paul taught that once we have come to Christ, we are to "Forget those things that are behind" (Phil. 3:13). He also said believers should "Reach for the things that are before . . ." (Phil. 3:13-14). Reaching is from a Greek word that means to "stretch oneself forward." It requires effort to reach for something. We should not sit and wait for God to move but should reach out and seize what God has for us. Repetitive cycles can remain broken, if we change our routines by replacing the cycle with renewal of God's word, prayer, and worship.

7 | CAN CHILDREN BE INFLUENCED BY DEMON SPIRITS?

Occasionally, the secular news will report the terrible tragedy of a mentally troubled parent who killed a child or their children, claiming they were "possessed by demons." These examples are a horrible excuse attempting to justify the tragedy, in hopes the murderer can be charged as "mentally incompetent" to stand trial. When more information is researched, the child may have had an autism, an emotion problem, or cried frequently. At times a selfish or impatient parent either willfully or ignorantly took the life of their child, claiming they were unable to bear the parental pressure caused by some physical or emotional dysfunctions. In reality the child was never possessed in any manner, yet ignorance caused a tragedy.

The questions we will delve into are: Can a child come under some form of demonic influence? If so, what type, and how can it be dealt with from a purely biblical manner?

In the Scripture, there are only two examples of children coming under demonic influence, and in both narratives a spirit was involved with a manifestation of serious *sickness* or *infirmity* in the child. One account in Matthew 17 was of a father whose son was having severe seizures. The lad would experience these terrible attacks whenever he was near water or when he was near a fire. While I am not a medical doctor, I have friends who before being healed or treated suffered from seizures that were often triggered by bright red lights that were flashing (fire often has flashes of red and orange). Water, especially reflecting in sunlight, can almost blind a person who is looking directly into the reflection. Some medical experts today would give an explanation as to why the red fire or the reflective water triggered these seizures. The father however, noted that once his son's seizures began, this infirm spirit would shake his body, attempting to throw his son into the burning flame or drown him in the water. It is clear this was not just a strange physical infirmity; this spirit was attempting to kill the little fellow by burning or drowning him.

The second example is recorded in Matthew chapter 15. Jesus was ministering along the coast of northern Israel when a Gentile women, a Canaanite, approached Him, begging Him to heal her daughter who was grievously (meaning badly or miserably) vexed by a devil (Matt. 15:22).

The word *vexed* (by a spirit) is used to describe the condition of the young boy and the woman's daughter (Matt. 15:22; 17:15). However, the Greek words are different. The word used when the boy was "vexed" is *pascho*, and refers to *a feeling, a sensation* of some form. The idea is this spirit suddenly comes upon him and makes him act in a certain manner (convulsing) or feel sensations he does not normally feel. The woman's daughter was "vexed," and this word *diamonizomai* is used for being exorcised by a demon. The woman's daughter was possessed by a spirit that was affecting her in some terrible manner. The lad with the seizures had not been born with them because when Christ asked how long was it since the spirit attacked him, the father said "of a child" (Mark 9:21). To certain Pharisees in Christ's day, these infirmities in the children were the result of some past sin in the life of a parent or a relative, and God was now punishing the parent by giving them a suffering child. I may add, this is *not a biblical view* and should be rejected.

In Christ's day, the religious Jews taught a tradition to explain why children were born with certain sicknesses. These traditions were so inbred that when the disciples came across a man born blind, they posed this question to Christ: "Who did sin, this man or his parents" (John 9:1-2). The question makes no rational sense. How could a man sin as an infant if he was *born* blind? In Christ's time, among the Greeks and the other religions throughout Asia, there was a strange belief in the transmigration of souls. This unbiblical theory taught that when a living person sins, at death their soul is sent from their body into another person's body to be punished for their past sins in a previous life. The reason the disciples asked this question is this theory was also known and believed by some philosophical Pharisees. In fact, Herod beheaded the righteous John the Baptist, later hearing of Christ's miracle ministry. Herod feared Christ was the reincarnation of John, who had come back from the dead and was now living in Christ's body (Mark 6:14). This is why when Christ asked His disciples, "Whom do men say that I am," they answered, "Some say . . . Jeremiah or one of the prophets" (Mark 1:14). Jeremiah the prophet had been dead for hundreds of years, yet the theory of transmigration was what some common people believed.

The Hindu religion still maintains the idea that the sin a person commits living in one body will be visited when the soul reenters another body, after that person dies. This is called reincarnation. Some of their beliefs are: A headache is allegedly punishment for speaking irreverently about your father or mother. Mental disorders are the alleged result of being disobedient to your parents, or your spiritual leader. Seizures are said to be the punishment for poisoning a person in your previous life. If your eyes hurt it's supposed to be the punishment for coveting another man's wife in your former life. Blindness is the punishment for a person having killed their mother while living in a former body. Such superstition only chains people with religious fear and keeps them in bondage to false thinking.

Christ made it clear "that neither this man nor his parents had sinned," but the man would become a manifestation of God's glory when Christ would heal him (John 9:3). Christ declared Himself the "light of the world," moments before sending this blind man, with mud balls in his eyes, to the pool of Siloam to wash and be healed

(John 9:5-7). The narrative of this blind man is significant as it illustrates the importance of not judging with false or man-made traditions the reason for a person's infirmity, but to focus on the cure, which is the healing power of Christ.

Solomon was anointed king in his Father David's place when he was about age twelve. It was Solomon who penned numerous Proverbs, when speaking about a child or children. He wrote, "Foolishness is bound in the heart of a child" (Prov. 22:15). He knew that the actions of a child will reveal early if the child's works (life) will be good or evil (Prov. 20:11). He knew that a child left to himself (or isolated from others) would eventually bring some form of shame upon his mother (Prov. 29:15). He understood that if you train up a child in the direction he should go, he would not depart from it (Prov. 22:6).

How Are Children Impacted by Sin?

Many years ago, while discussing the impact spirits have on children, a minister told me that when he was a young boy, there was a cousin who would sneak over to their house when his dad was at work to hang around some of the young girls. On one occasion he told this boy, "Come over to the barn and peep in and watch the show." The little fellow saw this teenager have sexual relations with the girls. Many years later, unable to remove the images from his mind, a door was opened for a spirit of pornography that could be traced back to the images carved into his brain that he had difficulty washing from the mainframe of his mind. Negative information and activity fed into a child's mind and spirit can impact them later in life.

Throughout the Scriptures, the adversary targeted infants and young men. The first premeditated murder in the Bible was when one brother, Cain, slew his younger brother, Abel, in a jealous rage (Gen. 4:1-13). From Satan's perspective, the motive may have been to destroy the firstborn son of Adam and slaying the righteous linage through Abel, to prevent the "seed of the woman" from crushing the head of the enemy (Gen. 3:15). With one son dead and the other under a curse, this was a double blow to the first family. Seth was Adam's third recorded son who carried on the righteous seed. Hundreds of years later, Joseph was destined to lead the Jewish family, but was nearly slain as a teenager by his own brothers, who chose instead to sell him as a slave. The reason for their animosity was jealousy of Joseph's dreams that revealed his future dominion over them (Gen. 37:19-27). Moving from Genesis to Exodus, we see the attempted murder of Hebrew infants after their birth (Exod. 1). According to Josephus, Pharaoh was warned by his Egyptian magicians that a child born among the Jews would bring down the Egyptian Empire. This became Pharaoh's motivation to slay all the sons born to the Hebrew women (Exod. 1:22). The same spirit of slaying the innocents was released upon Herod the Great, who appointed a small army of Roman soldiers to take the lives of all children under two years of age, in and around the Bethlehem region (Matt.

1:16-18), to prevent a newborn infant from becoming a future Jewish king.

Notice in these biblical references, the attacks were planned by wicked men and enacted outwardly against the infants and the youth. It seems the strategy of the dark kingdom against an infant is to prevent the child from *entering the world*, and against a young person it is to *destroy or prevent their destiny* from being fulfilled.

The two examples in the New Testament of children being assaulted by spirits both deal with some form of sickness or infirmity. It is important to note that not all sickness is caused by an infirm spirit or is demonically instigated. The main difference between an adult and a child is the adult has more knowledge and stronger willpower to resist or rebuke whatever is coming against them. On the other hand, a child has limited understanding, and needs the assistance of others to instruct them in all spiritual truth.

Demonic Movies

Years ago, I was ministering on a Sunday night in a large church in Ohio. Toward the conclusion of my message, a man jumped up and said, "Pray for my son! Pray for my son!" I spotted the lad, about ten years of age, laying across the church pew and was having what appeared to be a seizure. I laid down the microphone and ran into the congregation to the pew where the boy was shaking violently. I asked the father if this occurred often and he replied, "No, I have never seen him do this before!"

I thought this was rather odd, and knew that this was an attack caused by some type of spirit. I leaned over and demanded that in the name of Jesus this spirit release this boy. Within seconds, the shaking stopped and he returned to himself. Everyone began rejoicing, glorifying God for His delivering power.

After the service, I asked the father for details on what may have opened the door for this demonic incursion. The dad lowered his head, looking rather embarrassed, and said, "The other day we were watching the movie *The Exorcist*—you know, the one with the demon-possessed girl. My boy was also watching and became greatly afraid of what he saw and was worried a spirit could possess him. I guess this movie opened a door and the enemy saw his fear . . ." The lesson I learned is what children see can create fear and anxiety, which in return can open a crack in the door of their mind for spirits of fear and infirmity to violate their lives.

THE MOLESTATION OF THE INNOCENTS

One way in which unclean spirits can be transferred from one person to another is through sexual immorality, especially through forms of sexual abuse and molestation. When an individual commits a sin, such as lying, stealing, cheating, or coveting, the act may impact others, but in reality these acts of sin corrupts the person's spirit. When a child is sexually abused, the adversary will use mental triggers for years to come to recall the pain and fear of the childhood exploitation. Without healing of the hurtful memories and a renewed mind through Christ's redeeming power, those troublesome memories rise from the past, creating a marital rift, as accepting any affection may be met with a wall of resistance, and physical touch is interpreted as just being used for a sex object and not actually being loved. Since our childhood and youth are when and where our spiritual values are set for the remaining part of our lives, is it any wonder that Satanic armies of demons and men strategize for kids to see pornography at the average first-time age of eleven, to hook them for life. Drugs and alcohol are now consumed by kids in their pre-teen years, in hopes the addiction will tie their souls, for years to come, to the hands of dealers and distributors.

All forms of bondage often impact the one person under the grip of darkness. The reason that sins such as adultery or even homosexuality have such repercussions is that they involve more than one person. The Bible alludes to fornication between a man and a woman and says the "two become one flesh."

Herein lies an important point. In most cases if a spirit attaches itself to a child or young teen, it has been allowed in through doors of broken covenants, open sin, and willing disobedience that are opened by the sins of the family fathers, or by adults in the home whom themselves are living in bondages and are passing their familiar spirits around in the home. This transfer of spirits occurs easily, if there is not a true believer living in the house to restrain through prayer the forces of darkness. Paul alluded to a type of hedge when he wrote:

"For the unbelieving husband is sanctified by the wife, and the unbelieving wife is sanctified by the husband; otherwise your children would be unclean, but now they are holy."
—1 Corinthians 7:14

An early scholar, Adam Clark, commented on this unusual passage when he wrote:

> The Jews considered a child as born out of holiness whose parents were not proselytes at the time of the birth, though afterward they became proselytes. On the other hand, they considered the children of heathens born in holiness, provided the parents became proselytes before the birth. All the children of the pagans were reputed unclean by the Jews; and all their own children holy . . .

Paul's admonition in 1 Corinthians 7:12-16 indicates that if one of the parents in a house is a strong believer, then their spiritual influence could have an impact on their unsaved companions and their children would come under their spiritual covering. Jacob understood this principle when he prayed that the same angel that had been with him and blessed him would continue to follow his family, especially his two grandsons, Ephraim and Manasseh, who were born in Egypt and were adopted into the family of Israel:

> *"The Angel which redeemed me from all evil, bless the lads; and let*
> *my name be named on them, and the name of my fathers,*
> *Abraham and Isaac; and let them grow into a*
> *multitude in the midst of the earth."*
> —Genesis 48:16

There is a spiritual principle of transferring blessings from one generation to another (see Gen. 27 and 28). There is also a principle that the iniquities of the fathers can be passed to the third and fourth generation of those who are not serving the Lord (see Exod. 20:5). This principle can be seen when ministers will often see children, grandchildren, and great-grandchildren active in the church and ministry as this blessing continues from father to son and daughter. On the opposite end, this also explains how a family will have generations of drug addicts, alcoholics, sexual abuse, and other vices, as there is not a godly, redeemed, anointed leader in the family to restrain the entrance of an evil spirit.

DRUGS AND DEMONIC ACTIVITY

Two of the most bizarre stories I have ever heard were related to me by two men. Both are now ministers of the Gospel, and both were former drug abusers. One recalled smoking a dangerous type of mushroom with one of the buddies. He described how his vision became so distorted that everything he looked at became like a cartoon and would stretch and twist. They both were laughing, but the laughter stopped when he saw something coming toward him out of his fish tank. As he stared at this object, it took the form of a frightening demonic spirit that stood a few feet away. At first, he assumed the image was just another type of hallucination, until the supernatural being spoke in an audible voice saying, "Your mother's prayers are not helping you. Her prayers can't help you . . ." The fact was his mother was a strong Christian who prayed for him every day. He was in shock, when his friend turned to him and said, "Did you see that spirit that is standing in front of the fish tank?" Thus, it was not a drug-induced hallucination, but was a manifestation of a familiar spirit that entered a portal into the natural world, as the drug had opened up a center of the brain that tapped into the dangerous world of demons.

The second minister, before his conversion, was hooked on heroin and was with a large group of young people who were partying in California. That night he also saw a demon entity. The most stunning aspect of this manifestation was that there were about seven young people in the room. All had been raised in church but were in a backslidden condition, and every one of them saw the same demon appear at the same time. The chances of seven people, all backsliders, seeing the same exact spirit is virtually impossible.

Drugs are more than chemical substances used to dull

pain, alter the personality, or create creepy hallucinations. Illegal drugs in all forms are "gateway substances." Often, a lower form of a high leads a person to seek a higher high, or a slight dulling of the senses requires a stronger numbing sensation to block out all emotional misery.

ALTERING THE PERSONALITY

One of the worst effects of illegal drugs and alcohol (or drug abuse) is the altering effect it has on the personality of the person who consumes them. A gentle father will become a violent beast when he is drunk, and an honest child will steal from his mother and from friends to sustain their drug habit. When my own son was struggling with an addiction to DXM, I remember how he was not the same kid that his mother and I raised, and the drug made him either sleepy for long periods, agitated continually, or at times very depressed.

The New Testament warns against "sorcery" (Gal. 5:19-20; Rev. 18:23). The Greek word is *pharmakeia*, and can refer to magic (the type performed in Egypt in Exodus) and also to substances that can alter a person's personality. In certain Greek temples, men and women would visit the high priest or priestess who would allegedly be skilled in predicting the future. These were called the oracles and were usually performed after the priest would become slightly drunk with a wine mixture that was more of a drug. Similar mixtures were given to those who were greatly depressed and oppressed, temporarily relieving their pains. The real problem, however, was the individual could become addicted to the "relief" that was in the cup, pulling them back to the temple for another drink and another. Of course, the temple profited from the continuous business generated by these faithful "addicts."

MY DAD'S ENCOUNTER WITH AN INFIRM SPIRIT

Children have a special place in God's heart to the point that He has assigned angels to watch over them (Matt. 18:10). From a biblical perspective, spirits can attack a child with physical infirmities of certain kinds. However, the same power that sets adults free from demonic activity is the same authority that can and will relieve a child from a spirit of sickness or oppressive affliction.

As stated earlier, if a child or youth deals with demonic activity, it is often the result of a family member (or members) who is outside of the wall of God's covenant of protection and is living a lifestyle of sin that is keeping the door open for the fiery darts of the enemy to penetrate from the outside into the inside.

In my book *We are Not Finished Yet*, I relate a very strange and insightful story that occurred to my father, Fred Stone:

> In the early 1950's a son was born to the family of William and Nalva Stone named Kenny Edgar. Physically he looked healthy but as time passed the

family noticed he was unable to physically walk or sit up. Extensive medical examinations and X-rays indicated there was nothing visibly wrong to cause this infirmity. During this same time, the child would let out screams and double over in pain, which appeared to come from his chest area. At this time Fred was traveling and ministering, returning home occasionally between meetings. Nalva noticed that when Fred was present, holding the child, that little Kenny demonstrated no signs of pain in his body. He would rest peacefully in Fred's arms.

One evening Fred took the crying child from his mother and dad's room and took him to a little bunk bed where he was sleeping, holding Kenny on his chest. He would gently stoke the little fellow's back and quietly pray for him. After some time Fred experienced a full color vision. He saw a creature that looked like a man but its teeth and features were twisted. The color of its skin was a dull grey. The creature stood at the foot of the cot and suddenly thrust its hand into the chest area, near the heart of the child and twisted its hand. Instantly the infant began to jerk its body and scream in pain.

Fred rose up in bed, grabbing the child with his right arm and shoving his left hand out toward the spirit. He lunged toward it and yelled out, "You foul spirit, I command you to get your hands off this child in Jesus name." The spirit had a look of terror and stepped back about five feet. It replied to Fred, "I cannot do anything to this child while you are here, but you will be gone in three days and there is no one else like you in this house and when you are gone I will do what I want to." The creature evaporated from his sight. Fred grasped Kenny tight and continued praying for some time. Later that night the Lord gave him a spiritual dream. He recalls:

"In this dream I saw little Kenny lying between Mom and Dad in their bed. From the waist up Mom and Dad looked like humans but from the waist down they looked like a swine. I knew in the Bible a swine represented a spiritual backslider (2 Pet. 2:22). The Lord spoke to me and said, 'You must tell your mother and father that I have given them this child to be a blessing to them when they get old (Kenny was the youngest of twelve children). If they will serve me I will heal them, if not I will take him on. I want this child raised to follow me.'

"The next day I told mom and dad the dream. Dad cursed and said, 'Why would God take him when we decide how we want to live and he doesn't ? I answered him, 'Dad you will live to be old (he lived to be eighty-four) and Kenny will help take care of you, but God doesn't want him raised in a life of sin, and you and mom aren't serving God.'

"At that time, mother and dad did not repent and serve God. Thirty days later I received a call where I was preaching a revival that Kenney Edgar had died. Both of my parents were grieved, but months later they received Christ in one of my revivals!"

At that time my father was serving Christ and ministering. The presence of Christ in him was also effective to restrain the presence of this infirm spirit. In His mercy the Lord took the little lad to prevent him from suffering. Years later Dad's parents accepted the Lord and passed away in a good old age.

The revelations within this story are amazing. God gives us children to care for us as we get older. Secondly, God can take a child when it is young if it sees the child is going to be raised in sin or the parents are living in sin. This is not judgment but mercy and ensures that the infant enters the kingdom. Thirdly, God is able to bring healing and deliverance based upon the spiritual obedience of the parents. The child needed deliverance, and at that time the personal sins in the house kept the door opened to this spiritual attack.

In summary, children are greatly favored by God and are watched over by angels. Children born in a home where at least one of the parents has a salvation covenant is under the hedge of that parent as children. When both parents are living in sin, doors can open for assaults from various spirits within the home. Any spirit that attacks the mind of a child can be expelled through faith in the power of Christ's name and the delivering authority in the Holy Spirit. Children with Christian parents must be taught not to fear any type of evil spirit, but to believe that God has given them angels to protect them. Christian parents should also pray for favor and blessing over their children.

8 | BELIEVERS IN THE EYES OF THE ADVERSARY

I have more than 15,000 books in my personal library, the majority with religious content. Of the thousands of spiritual warfare books that I have read, the majority expose Satan's strategies, teach believers how to overcome temptation or trials, or generally provide insight into the who, what, when, where, and how of warfare. Most authors examine the enemy through the lens of God's Word, peppered with illustrations of believers who overcame all forms of adversity. None I have read, however, explored how believers are viewed *through the eyes of the devil*, or answer how Satan perceives Christ, the church, or us, individually, once we have been made a new creation in Christ. This chapter will delve into this thought.

Numerous believers prefer to avoid all conversations related to demonic activity or Satan, as there is a pre-conceived idea that by exposing the depths of Satan's kingdom and how to deal with him, their illumination will only open doors to unwanted warfare. For example, Paul wrote to the Hebrew believers informing them that their persecution for receiving Christ as the Messiah was a result of their illumination; their mental understanding being opened to truth (Heb. 10:32). However, ignoring the enemy for fear of a conflict actually creates a false security. Some think that if a believer never talks about anything negative, or exposes the truth behind fallen angels, demons, and the devil, they instantly default from warfare and the adversary will never find them on his radar; thus, no threat means no battles. It was Paul who admonished the church to not be "ignorant of his (the Devil's) devices" (2 Cor. 2:11). Therefore, ignorance could get you spiritually killed while knowledge can save your soul and your life. The first step is to understand how Satan views the Commander of our Faith, Jesus Christ!

HOW SATAN NOW VIEWS JESUS

Christianity is a faith identified by non-Christians through its symbolism. When anyone outside the Christian faith, with even limited religious understanding, sees a person with a cross dangling on a gold chain around their neck, their immediate thought is, "They must be a Christian." In fact, the cross representing Christ is so offensive to Muslims that when our soldiers fought in the Gulf War, the Saudi leaders demanded that all Christian soldiers remove their cross necklaces or hide them under their shirt. Worldwide, the cross is the main symbol of the Christian faith, and to my knowledge no other religion uses this specific emblem. Throughout the world, the tall steeples towering at the entrances of older cathedrals and churches are marked at their highest point with gold- or silver-colored crosses. In some European countries, the emblem goes beyond a cross to small icons or metals worn as necklaces of Mary holding the infant Christ.

Satan, however, is not threatened or intimidated viewing millions of our silver- and gold-plated religious symbols, as holding a cross in someone's face does not frighten a demon (as implied in some movies), but the authority released through the *spoken name of Jesus* echoes fear within the kingdom of darkness. Christians joyfully grin when seeing a plastic or ceramic infant Jesus lying in a manger or resting in a plastic Mary's arms. I assure you, the adversary no longer views Christ as an innocent, helpless infant needing his mother's protection. Neither does he visualize Christ hanging from a splintered wooden cross in Jerusalem—as it was the cross that "paid the price" for redemption and the resurrection that "cashed the check," making what was available applicable! The cross without the resurrection would have been only half of God's redemption plan completed. Paul taught that without the resurrection our faith would be in vain (1 Cor. 15:12-14). What Satan sees is the *aftermath* of Calvary—the finished work of Christ.

THE AFTERMATH OF CALVARY

What Satan sees when he recalls Christ's finished work—the death and resurrection—is illustrated in an alleged story of Napoleon, the French military genius who lost the battle at Waterloo and was afterwards taken prisoner. It is said that a map was brought to him with a red spot marking Waterloo to remind him it was there that he lost his battle. The alleged statement, as he pointed his finger to the spot, was, "Little red dot, if it wasn't for you I would have won the war." In the eyes of Satan, every time he views a small hillside in Jerusalem called Golgotha, he is reminded, "Little hill, if it wasn't for the red blood of Christ spilled upon you I could have ruled the world!" While the world sees Christ upon the cross in paintings, in movies, and on millions of tiny fourteen karat gold crucifixes, Satan recalls an empty tomb in an ancient garden outside the limestone walls of Jerusalem where the seed of the woman (Christ) gave him a permanent bruise on the head (Gen 3:15).

Christ is no longer an infant but a fully grown, resurrected Savior. I believe Satan's continuous imagery is the same that the Apostle John observed in Revelation 1:12-17. John saw Christ's eyes flash like a burning fire, as His hair glistened white like snow while His feet appeared like polished brass having been burned in a furnace. John was overwhelmed by Christ's facial radiance, which was as bright as the burning sun. This is not Christ the *infant* but Christ the *immortal*! If you have ever heard of someone "playing the devil's advocate," the devil positions himself as an attorney in the heavenly court, continually accusing believers before God (see Rev. 12:10). However, when the adversary introduces his false claims, he must encounter the greatest defense attorney (advocate—1 John 2:1) in the universe, our High Priest Christ Jesus (Heb. 8:1-3). As our advocate Christ has never lost a case in the heavenly court! Everyone who approaches the Judge (God), pleading guilty and seeking forgiveness, is released from the prison house of the enemy! When Satan attempts to accuse a forgiven believer, he cannot pass through the blood covering that surrounds a forgiven person. Satan wants God to see the *sin*, but God sees the *blood* of Messiah. Just as in the Exodus narrative, when God "saw the blood," he said, "I will pass over you" (Exod. 12:13). When the heavenly Father sees the blood of His son applied to your soul, His judgment against you will pass over you and leave you justified by faith, cleared of guilt! When alluding to Christ, many see a cross; however, Satan sees a High Priest he cannot challenge.

HOW SATAN VIEWS THE CHURCH

When I say the word *church*, in the West, many visualize a physical sanctuary, a group of people worshipping in a home study or a denomination. The musically gifted may picture an orchestra, a praise and worship team, or a robed choir. However, a brick building and wooden altar benches in and of itself is not a threat to any demonic force; neither is a dry congregation of half-sleeping, Sunday-go-to-meeting church members who would rather be golfing at the country club than listening to a thirty-minute sermonette each Sunday.

As Christians, if we live in the West and say the word

church, most people visualize a local congregation where your name is inscribed on the membership rolls, or a major denominational headquarters that we grew up in. Satan, however, sees more than a building filled with people. He has a worldview and not just local vision. Every second on earth, he must deal with the universal Body of Christ—the hundreds of millions from all nations scattered around the globe whose names are inscribed in heaven and whose "membership" in the heavenly Kingdom consists of a "number which no man can number" (Rev. 7:9). For most, church is a central building, a believer's gathering place in our hometown, but from the upper atmosphere where Satan is the prince of the air (Eph. 2:2), he can view the underground church in China, the large 150,000-member church in Indonesia, the fastest-growing congregations covering Brazil and Latin America, and the countless Muslim youth secretly turning to Christ in Muslim nations! You may recognize the two hundred members or attendees of your local home church, but the prince of darkness must deal with a possible 1.5 billion (or more) individuals who, if they are truly believers, are living their lives mimicking Christ in word, deed, and power.

Satan already has knowledge of the prediction of his doom as foretold in the Bible. In the middle of the tribulation, Satan will come down with great wrath, "knowing he has a short time" (Rev. 12:12). His obituary has been penned in the Apocalypse, sealing his final destination in the lake of fire (Rev. 20:10). He also is alerted to the fact that there is an "army in heaven" that will be joining Christ in reclaiming the earth from the Antichrist's dominion and assisting Christ at the Armageddon Campaign (Rev. 16:16), ending with the eternal deportation of the Beast, False Prophet, and Satan himself (Rev. 19:11-14; 19:20). When the adversary and his hordes of wicked spirits peer into the future, they have advanced information and dread their future—a bottomless pit for a thousand years (Rev. 20:1-3) and a lake of fire for eternity (Rev. 20:10). We see people and buildings when we think "church," but when Satan thinks "church" he sees a kingdom.

HOW SATAN VIEWS AN INDIVIDUAL BELIEVER

It is common for one believer to see the weakness or faults in another believer, while ignoring their own. It is also easy to say we *forgive* but we never *forget*. When Satan sees an individual believer, he may know their weakness, their past sins, and realize there are cracks in doors that can permit him limited access into their lives. However, he also sees the blood of Christ that has erased their sinful past applied when they confessed Christ as their redeemer. Revelation 12:11 says, "They overcame (Satan) by the blood of the lamb and by the word of their testimony . . ." The precious blood of Christ has unlimited power over all the powers of the enemy. The accuser cannot accuse a person whose sins no longer exists in the eyes of God (Isa. 43:25), specifically sins that have been erased by the blood of Christ (Rev. 7:14). In Exodus 12, during the first Passover, the fearful angel of destruction was unable to cross the three-fold blood marks, applied three places on the outside lintel of the Hebrew homes. While you can choose whom you will serve, and willfully walk out from under God's protective covering, those who will abide in the secret place of the Most High (see Psalm 91), abiding in the Lord's Word, will remain under Christ's shield of blood.

This blood covenant covering provided by Christ is so intriguing to the spirit world that angelic messengers out of curiosity often seek to examine the activity encompassing the work of the Holy Spirit and His redemptive ability. We read:

"To them it was revealed that, not to themselves, but to us they were ministering the things which now have been reported to you through those who have preached the gospel to you by the Holy Spirit sent from heaven—things which angels desire to look into."
—1 Peter 1:12 (NKJV)

In the context of this verse, Peter is speaking about how the prophets diligently searched the Scriptures to unlock the concealed mystery of the time the Messiah would suffer (see Isa. 53) and would be glorified. Now that the Messiah has been revealed, angels have great interest to look into God's redemptive plan that transforms men from darkness to light. The angelic hosts now serve as the ministering spirits for the advancement of God's kingdom (Heb. 1:14). In ages past, this same heavenly kingdom was divided by an internal rebellion and an attempted overthrow of God by Satan and a third of his angelic following (Rev. 12:1-4). This sin of these angels is unforgivable without any promise of restoration through redemption. The two-thirds that remained loyal to God witnessed an earth-shaking sin failure in Eden, after Adam and Eve were created, when the couple were expelled from God's earthly garden, forever banished from the Tree of Life, and separated from God's intimate fellowship. However, this man-woman creation, formed in God's image, were given a second chance to redeem their souls from death through blood offerings (in the Old Testament), and eventually every living human in the world would be given a choice by being offered a plan of restoration through the blood of Christ. *Fallen angels were forever banished, while banished mankind could be forever forgiven.*

SATAN IS DEFEATED BY THOSE WHO KNOW THEIR SPIRITUAL AUTHORITY

In Acts 19:13-15, seven sons of a man called Sceva made a failed attempt to cast out spirits from a possessed man. We read:

> *Then some of the itinerant Jewish exorcists took it upon themselves to call the name of the Lord Jesus over those who had evil spirits, saying, "We exorcise you by the Jesus whom Paul preaches." Also there were seven sons of Sceva, a Jewish chief priest, who did so. And the evil spirit answered and said, "Jesus I know, and Paul I*

know; but who are you?"

The spiritual success of Paul and the failure of these seven sons to deal with these evil spirits is summed up in the *spiritual authority* delegated through a covenant relationship. Paul was a God ordained Apostle with apostolic power and authority exercising dominion over evil spirits; using Christ's delegated authority given to believers, as we read, "In my name you shall cast out devils . . ." (Mark 16:17), and "I give you power over all the power of the enemy" (Luke 10:19). Paul was in a personal relationship with Christ, whereas the seven sons had no relationship with Christ, but were approaching this possessed man using a formula; "Jesus whom Paul preaches." The demon within this demonized man knew who Jesus and Paul were, but mocked the command given by these men, when the spirit questioned them with the words, "but who are you?"

Authority is not something a person pronounces upon themselves. In the military, there are protocols followed when higher-ranking officers enter a room where there are lower-level soldiers. If a five-star general walks in, all lesser-ranked men (and women) are to stand at attention, salute, addressing him and answering him with "Sir!" God's kingdom also operates on certain authority principles recorded in a book of protocols called the Bible. God works within the bounds of Scripture whose inspired words reveal His promises and commandments. Breaking military protocols can get a soldier in serious trouble with those in authority over him (or her). The same is true when breaking the instruction and requirements of the New Covenant penned in the Word of God.

Authority gives the one bearing it certain control over those who are not given an equal measure. Here's a simple example. I was raised in a denomination that provided three levels of ministry credentials: The Exhorter, Licensed, and Ordained Bishop certification, each with certain requirements for entry and each with different levels of benefit. The Exhorter level recognized the younger ministers as God called preachers of the Gospel. This was determined by personal interviews with the state board and through oral and written tests examining a candidate's biblical knowledge. Basically, an Exhorter certificate gave a minister recognition and approval by older or senior ministers in the church. The next level, Licensed, enabled the minister to legally perform marriages and minister the sacraments to believers in the church. The Ordained level gave all the previous benefits, plus special voting rights during major conventions and the opportunity to serve as a bishop overseeing a state. Only an ordained bishop could be elected to a higher position called the Executive Committee and Executive Counsel. At age seventeen, through the ministry leadership in Virginia, I received recognition as an Exhorter. This was followed at age eighteen by the level of a Licensed minister; I was one of the youngest Licensed ministers in the denomination's state's history. Upon receiving this "official" certification, I also agreed to *submit* to all those who were "over me" in the

Lord (see Heb. 13:17). The presiding bishops in each state had the authority to revoke any of these three levels of recognition if they deemed it necessary through heretical teaching or a proven moral failure. Thus, a presiding bishop was one with years of experience and authority over those who were licensed and the exhorters, and those licensed were given different benefits not available to an exhorter. Experience, knowledge, and time could promote a minister into a different level of ministry, which also expanded his authority. Paul certainly taught this level of authority when he warned not to place a "novice" in a position of authority, to prevent pride from entering his heart (1 Tim. 3:6).

Christ's authority is like the roots of a tree buried deep in the ground that provides nourishment to all the branches. The power, life, and strength of any tree begins in the roots, but the life force that produces the fruit flows *from the roots* into all of the branches. One branch gives us authority over *sin*, to live a life free from the bondage and control of a sin nature, producing from this branch the fruit of righteousness. Another branch releases authority over *sickness and disease*, meaning that by exercising prayer in the name of Jesus and through a yoke-breaking anointing (Isa. 10:27), the diseases afflicting the body can be broken off the person seeking freedom. The fruit from this branch is health. Jesus gave His disciples authority over sickness, saying, "You shall lay hands upon the sick and they shall recover" (Mark 16:18). Another branch on this tree of spiritual authority gives the recipient the right to exercise authority over demons, including to expel them from the bodies of those under their dominion (those demon possessed). This act of exorcism is called "casting out devils" (Mark 16:17). In the Gospels the Greek word for "casting out" is *ekballo*, and is a strong word meaning *to thrust something out by force.* It is not a suggestion to the demons, like "You better leave this person alone. I'm going be upset and have to ask you to leave!" The word *ekballo* is a forceful command, a demand, and not a request that reveals the verbal authority a believer has to force an evil spirit out of the body of a person desiring freedom. This is the branch on God's family tree producing the fruit of deliverance.

The adversary wants to keep believers ignorant of their authority, giving them a sense of weakness against his wicked kingdom, deceiving them to question, "Who am I to come against such strong spirits?" First, you are not using *your authority* or *your* righteousness in this battle. You are personally representing the Messiah, demonstrating His authority, as it flows through the branches of this spiritual tree. It may be *your* voice rebuking the spiritual adversaries, but it is Christ Himself backing up and confirming the words you are speaking over the enemy. When you say, "Get behind me, Satan," Christ is demanding, "You heard them; do it right now!" When you resist the adversary with a verbal command, Christ is saying, "You heard them; leave them alone," as it is written that if you "resist the devil he will flee from you" (James 4:7).

Your "legal" authority provided through Christ can

be forfeited if the believer drops out of the race, lays down their protective armor of God, or steps outside the defensive boundary of God's covenant. A dear minister friend went through a horrible series of battles, with deadly diseases that struck his family, church members who turned against him, and a divorce from his wife. During this time, he became angry at God and said, "I quit, because you have let me down." He stepped out of the ministry and for the next several years lived a life without serving the Lord or ministering. During this time, he was on a mental and spiritual battlefield in which every day the enemy was beating up on him. Thankfully, he was restored and has returned to the pulpit. Under such situations when a believer willfully walks away from God's covenant, they also walk away from assigned spiritual protection, from blessing and favor, as all spiritual blessing are released on the condition of abiding in the faith (John 15:4, 7).

If I *quit* believing the Word or obeying God, or choose to turn back from the faith, I surrender to the enemy and *forfeit my authority*. During any war when opposing soldiers surrender, they are not released back into freedom by their captors. War prisoners are not provided a penthouse suite to spend time treating their battle wounds. They are normally put into a prisoner of war camp surround by high walls and barbed wire, fed meagerly, and given no contact information or ability to communicate outside their prison compound. Surrendering forces you to give up your weapons, which is your key to fight. I have spoken to individuals who turned from their faith and severed their fellowship with God. They ended up over time in terrible bondages, wrecked marriages, and lost opportunities, only to return to church years later blaming God for all of their heartache and trials. This would be like crashing your car after driving ninety miles an hour, surviving, and blaming the gas you purchased for the speed you were doing.

Like any spiritual promise of blessing, a believer must have confidence in their prayers and believe God is working in agreement with them when they exercise spiritual authority. Our legal rights to exercise authority over all the power of the enemy must be put into operation through action, through speaking the Word, and through obedience. Many believers treat their authority like a deer hunter from West Virginia or Kentucky who enters deer hunting season by calling his friends over to look at his new gun, with a powerful scope, hanging on the wall. There he sits by the fireplace, avoiding the cold weather outside and bragging, "Check out this new gun! The range is unbelievable and the scope is the best made in the world." As other hunters smile and exit the house, the man sits in his easy chair drinking coffee admiring his gun! Never exercising authority is like a deer hunter having a weapon on display that is never used.

AUTHORITY IS NOT A REQUEST—BUT A DEMAND

I was eighteen years of age when I encountered my first demon-possessed person, during an altar invitation at a state church convention in Roanoke, Virginia. A young man answered the altar call and I, along with other young ministers, serving on the altar committee, were "trained" to minister to any seekers coming forward. This particular "seeker" had never been in an altar and was controlled by an evil spirit that immediately began manifesting verbally with vile profanity. We began praying for him, when suddenly the fellow fell backwards, slithering like a snake. His eyes began rolling back and his voice changed. I began telling this spirit that it needed to come out of its victim . . . but to no avail. He was becoming violent, and as I leaned over him, to pray, he reached for my throat, popping the top button off my nice white shirt, while at the same time yanking on my tie. I knew I was *in trouble* and needed assistance from other ministers.

I left the scene and ran to the platform to call on the help of the presiding bishop, M. H. Kennedy, a seasoned and wise minister. I told him there was a fellow wallowing on the floor with a demon so strong no one could get it out. The bishop looked me over, shook his head, and slowly made his way to the location, greeting ministers along the way. When arriving, I was anticipating a Mount Carmel type showdown—the demon verses M. H. Kennedy, "live" in Roanoke, Virginia! Instead, Kennedy stared down the young man whose lips were pouring out horrible profanity, when suddenly Kennedy's eyes met the young man and Kennedy yelled, "I command you in the name of Jesus Christ to come out of this man!" Immediately the fellow's body when limp. Kennedy yelled, "Now get up and rejoice—you're delivered." We helped him up and he immediately raised his hands, shouting that he was free. I stood there wet with perspiration, my hair disheveled, a button missing from my shirt and my tie twisted, somewhat stunned. I thought, "Why could not we cast this out?"

Years later Kennedy was assigned a church in Jessup, Georgia, and he invited me to conduct a revival. I asked him if he remembered the Roanoke incident and he laughed, saying he remembered and also recalled what I looked like when I approached him. I asked him why he thought that I had failed in seeing the fellow delivered from this spirit. He asked me to review the entire incident. After a discussion he said, *"You were too passive, as though you were asking the spirit to come out, and I was using spiritual authority, demanding the demon to come out."* This brief discussion explained a point I have never forgotten, that verbal authority spoken against evil spirits is not a *request* but a *demand*. When Jesus said to legion in the man of Gedera, "Come out" (Mark 5:8), it was not "Come out if you are ready to," or "Come out if you want to," or "Come out or I'm coming in to get you." Christ demanded and commanded these spirits to depart, and the results speak for themselves. The man was freed—sitting, clothed, and in his right mind (Mark 5:15).

Believers have authority to *rebuke* and *resist* the devil. If we rebuke and do not resist, we weaken our wall of resistance and the adversary enters through cracks in our wall. If we resist and don't rebuke, we limit the influence of our authority, as authority in the Bible was always released by speaking and not just doing. When Jesus cast out spirits He used His words, and people observed, "With authority he commands even the unclean spirits and they do obey him" (Mark 1:27). Rebuking is verbal and resisting requires action. Rebuking is what Christ did when He was tempted of Satan and quoted Scriptures that countered Satan's temptations. Resisting is an act—a refusal to do what is suggested. Jesus refused to turn stones to bread, refused to jump from the pinnacle of the temple, and refused to bow to Satan (Matt. 4:1-10). This is "resisting" the devil. Resisting prevents *you* from acting and rebuking prevents *Satan* from acting (James 4:7). Resisting and rebuking are strengthened by the Scriptures. The Scriptures are both an offensive and defensive weapon; offensive in that they have power to invade the enemy's territory and take back what has been seized, and defensive in that when they are believed, they can withstand any weapon Satan throws at them. Authority frees you, and resisting Satan keeps you free.

Most Christians have several Bibles in their homes: one in the living room, one by the nightstand, and others tucked in drawers or collecting dust in an office. For too many, this sacred covenant book is treated like a Gideon's Bible in a hotel drawer. It's available, but only pulled out and read when they are bored, or when a person needs something from God. It reminds me of the person whom the doctor has warned for years, "You must exercise to keep your heart healthy or you will have a heart attack in the future." This person purchases an expensive treadmill they never use (too busy to take time), purchases books on healthy eating that remain on the shelf, and continues their routine—until years later they have a heart attack. Then they decide it's time to dust off the books and change their lifestyle—only after the damage had been done.

That brown leather-covered Bible with black ink and the words of Jesus in red is not for the purpose of decorating your house like a flower arrangement on the coffee table or some beautiful painting to be admired. Neither is it some form of a mystical device that restrains evil spirits when they see it on your nightstand. You can polish the cover, run your hands over the pages, and hug a Bible because of your love for the Word. But the words must be secured in your heart and spoken from your mouth. The Bible says:

"But what does it say? 'The word is near you, in your mouth and in your heart' (that is, the word of faith which we preach): that if you confess with your mouth the Lord Jesus and believe in your heart that God has raised Him from the dead, you will be saved. For with the heart one believes unto righteousness, and with the mouth confession is made unto salvation."
—Romans 10:8-10 (NKJV)

The Bible is your legal document, proving and promising your access to authority. Your heart is the storage vault and your mouth is the door that opens to the hidden treasure concealed within. Satan would love you ignorant of your spiritual authority as God's people can perish for lack of knowledge.

THE SPIRIT AND A BODY PRINCIPLE

James wrote that the "body without the spirit is dead" (James 2:26). We all consist of an eternal spirit, with a soul dwelling in a body (1 Thess. 5:23). Without a body, my spirit has no voice to speak on earth, as without my spirit my body is dead, since death occurs when the spirit is absent from the body (2 Cor. 5:6-8). This "body-spirit" principle is true in the entire spirit world. Adam was a dust body lying on the ground until God breathed the "breath of life," which raised him to life as a "living soul" (Gen. 1:27). When Satan initiated his plan to deceive Eve, he did not appear in his normal form as the fallen angel, as this appearance would have been too obvious and he would have been exposed as an unwelcomed intruder in the garden. Instead, he used a "body" of a subtle creature—a serpent (Gen. 3:1)—as without a "body" he would have been illegal in God's garden.

When God wanted to manifest His will on the earth He always found a man—a king, priest, or prophet—to proclaim His voice—his message—on the earth. On a few occasions God spoke audibly to prophets such as Abraham and Moses, and to kings: Saul, David, and Solomon. However, during the majority of occasions, the prophet would announce with His voice, "Thus saith the Lord." The Holy Spirit would "come upon" judges and leaders, inspiring them in times of crisis, war, and important decision making.

When God desired to bring redemption, He sent His beloved son, Jesus Christ, in a human body to personally represent Him on the earth and reveal His plan and process of redemption. When Christ spoke, it was God speaking, and when He performed miracles, it was God working. When Christ ascended to heaven He promised to send "another comforter," the Holy Spirit (John 14:16, 26). However, the Holy Spirit required a "body" in which to operate in the earth. Therefore, the Holy Spirit enters the body of believers and through His authority He releases the power of God to touch others in need!

On the Day of Pentecost, 120 people were individually filled with the Spirit. Each person received their own infilling. However, as a collective group this new organism called the "church" (Matt. 16:18; 18:17) became the "Body of Christ" on the earth (1 Cor. 12:27), with each believer serving as one member on this global body. The body of Christ covers the earth, and when united becomes an unstoppable force that wreaks chaos on the kingdom of darkness as they shine the Gospel light into the face of all spiritual opposition. The church is Christ's body on earth and the Holy Spirit dwells in that body, giving the church legal authority on earth to challenge the kingdom of darkness.

THE ORIGIN OF THE EKKLESIA

In the English version of the Bible the word *church*—singular—is found seventy-seven times in seventy-six verses, and *churches*—plural—is used thirty-seven times in thirty-six verses. By definition, the church is an institution established by Christ for those who receive and sustain a covenant relationship with Him. The Greek word for *church* is *ekklesia*, meaning the "called out ones" or those who are "called out of this world's system into the kingdom of God." The word *ekklesia* comes from two Greek words: *ek* (out of) and *kleh'o* (to call).

In my youth I assumed Christ originated this word. However, this word was known and used in Greece and among the Greeks. The *ekklesia* was a political term for an assembly of citizens, who were called forth into the main part of the city by a blast of a trumpet. Once they were gathered they became an assembly of united citizens— one unit. This assembly held the ultimate power over any form of government that arose, including voting power. In Athens they were summoned by law four times every thirty-six or thirty-seven days, or about forty times a year. The assembly voted on the laws, the leaders, and all the political decisions of the city in the Greek state. If the city government became corrupt or lawless, these *ekklesia* could reject them and collapse the government within one day, as they had the authority to elect or remove any official working within the state. It was Christ who used this known political word to describe the authority He was releasing within His spiritual kingdom. This is why, after He said He would "build my church," (Matt. 16:18), He then in the next verse gave believers incredible spiritual authority by promising:

"And I will give you the keys of the kingdom of heaven, and whatever you bind on earth shall be bound in heaven, and whatever you loose on earth shall be loosed in heaven."
—Matthew 16:17 (NJKV)

In Christ's *ekklesia*, there is a King (Christ), a Judge (God the Father), and an Administrator (the Holy Spirit). The common people in Christ's day soon began perceiving Him as a candidate for the king of Israel and eventually the king over the earthly kingdoms. They knew He could heal them and feed them and they desired to promote Him to a political position of king (John 6:15). Near Passover, they threw palm branches down as He rode a donkey into Jerusalem (Matt. 21:9), crying out "Hosanna," meaning "Lord save now," as though begging Him to seize authority over their Roman oppressors. Shortly after this, Christ stood at His trial before the High Priest and the counsel, where they did not question Him on His possible Messianic position but demanded to know if He was the King of Israel. This king theme climaxed at the crucifixion, where Pilate wrote an inscription on the cross, Jesus of Nazareth the King of The Jews (John 19:19). After His resurrection and before His ascension, the disciples inquired if Christ would soon "restore the kingdom to Israel" (Acts 1:7). The people and the disciples saw a king and a kingdom, not just a messiah and a savior.

The Greek word *ekklesia* is derived from another Greek word, *ek-kaleo*, (pronounced *ek-leh'o*). This word is used when speaking of calling forth, such as a king calling forth his army. This is what Christ will do when He pre-pares to return to earth as the "king of kings." He will call forth His heavenly army, who will follow Him upon white horses (Rev. 19:14-16).

This calling forth principle is found in the life of Moses. According to the Bible, as an infant Moses was discovered by Pharaoh's daughter, floating in a small, protective ark. He was adopted by her and raised in the palace of Pharaoh. As an adult he became a political-military leader. Josephus the Jewish historian said Moses led a battle defeating the king of Ethiopia, marrying the king's daughter, and bringing her back to Egypt. Years later, he slew an Egyptian, fled for his life to a desert in Median, where he connected with Jethro, marrying one of his daughters and becoming a lone shepherd in the desert for forty years (Exod. chapter 1 and 2).

One afternoon while enduring the routine of watching sheep, he received an unexpected life-changing visitation from heaven, through a burning bush, where God instructed him to return back to Egypt and demand Pharaoh to let the Hebrew people go free (see Exod. 3 and 4). Moses experienced an *ek'kaleo* (a call) to bring forth the nation (the *ekklesia*) and assemble them by "bringing them forth" out of their bondage into their Promised Land. During Israel's early journey in the wilderness, when Moses was on the mountain forty days receiving the Law of God, the people sinned by molding and worshipping a golden calf. There were twelve tribal Fathers—and the tribe of Levi stood against this idolatry. Thus, God separated this tribe to become the priests in Israel at the Tabernacle and the Temple. They were thus "called out" ones that were separated within the called-out nation— Israel (see Exod. 32).

ON EARTH AS IN HEAVEN

In the Lord's Prayer, Christ taught to pray, "Thy will be done in earth as it is in heaven" (Matt. 6:10). The will of God for you and me is prearranged and set in heaven, even prior to our birth. Every person born on earth is pre- known to God, as when the Lord told Jeremiah, "Before I formed you in the womb, I knew you, before you were born I sanctified you; I ordained you to be a prophet to the nations" (Jer. 1:5). In some instances, God went as far as to name the child before it was born. King Cyrus was named about 150 years before he came to birth (Isa. 44:28). Josiah, Jesus, and John were all named before their births (1 Kings 13:2). We were known from the beginning of time, as the Bible speaks of names being written in heaven from the foundation of the world (Rev. 17:8).

God's plan is known from the *foundation* of the world, as Christ is called the "lamb slain from the foundation of the world" (Rev. 13:8), and "foreordained before the foun- dation of the world" (1 Pet. 1:19-20). Christ spoke of the Father's love toward Him "before the foundation of the world" (John 17:24). The phrase "the foundation of the world" refers to the very beginning of creation (Gen. 1:1). The kingdom of heaven was also prepared for us from the foundation of the word:

"Come, you blessed of My Father, inherit the kingdom prepared for
you from the foundation of the world."
—Matthew 25:34-35

According to the Scripture, there is a pre-set foreordained will of God set in advance in heaven that must manifest on the earth. To experience this manifestation, we must "call forth" the will of God to be done on earth as it is in heaven. Your obedience can speed up or disobedience can delay the will of God. For example, it was God's will to bring Israel into the Promised Land when they departed from Egypt. Normally, this would have been a two-week journey by foot if they followed the Mediterranean Sea route. Instead it became a forty-year mess of walking around in circles in a hot desert, as their unbelief *delayed the will of God for one generation* (Psa. 95:10).

God directed Jonah to Nineveh, to warn the city of God's impending judgment if they did not repent. Instead, Jonah chose a self-invited "cruise" on the Mediterranean to avoid ministering to a city of Assyrians whom he despised. His disobedience delayed God's objective, but God won out when He sent Jonah on a pre-arranged "submarine ride" in the belly of a giant fish. When Jonah escaped from the fish he made up for lost time, reducing the three-day journey to Nineveh to only one day (Jonah 1-2).

It is through our prayers and confessions made with

our mouth that we call the will of God out of heaven into the earth and through obedience we see that Divine will manifested. A good illustration is how I met my future wife, Pam. As a young teenager I had met several young Christian girls that I thought could be possible candidates for marriage. Yet, in each case, something eventually occurred that severed the relationship. After breaking off one relationship, I was praying for God's *perfect*—not His *permissible*—will to be done (see Rom. 12:2). The phrase "perfect will" in Romans 12:2 literally means the *complete* or *completed* will of God. In January 1980, I sought direction for the perfect will of God for my future, thirty days later, in February, I met Pam Taylor, whom I was irresistibly drawn to, and I received an inspiration in my spirit that she was to be my wife. The inner feeling was so clear that I had no doubt I would marry her. After two years of "dating by phone," I finally received the boldness to ask her to spend her life with me as my companion. She has been much more to me and our two children than I could have ever imagined. In February 1980, it was God's perfect will for me to preach a four-week revival at her home church in Northport, Alabama, allowing me meet her and get to know her. Christ taught us to pray that God's will be done "on earth." Using our spiritual authority, we are given the ability to call things that are not as though they already were (Rom. 4:17).

Once you are converted to Christ and enter the kingdom, you must learn to exercise this kingdom authority over the challenges you face in life and in restraining the forces of the adversary from instigating their will or dark plans in your life. You must call in the will of God and not just maintain status quo, but grow in the grace and knowledge of the Lord Jesus Christ.

9 | How Unclean Spirits Are Expelled From a Person

The belief in demonic possession existed long before the ministry of Christ. King Saul was tormented by an evil spirit of jealousy, motivating him with an obsession to slay David. Only when David played on his harp in the presence of the king was Saul made well. The Bible says Saul was "refreshed." The Hebrew word for "refreshed" is *ravach* and means "revive or to breath freely," and by implication means to have an ample or enlarged room. A person under demonic control often stays to themselves, alone in small, cramped rooms living in the dark. Everything feels as though it is closing in on them. Once refreshed and made well, they initiate communication with family and friends. They get out of their oppressive space and go outdoors to enjoy life.

Some Spirits Are More Stubborn

In one New Testament narrative, Christ's nine disciples confronted a spirit in a young boy that was causing painful seizures. After the disciples prayed, rebuking the spirit, they became disappointed when they saw the spirit seemed to ignore their rebuke and remain in the body of its victim. Jesus, along with Peter, James, and John, descended off a mountain and saw the confusion caused by the failed deliverance. Jesus took control and the spirit was immediately exorcised from the lad. When the nine disciples inquired as to why they could not cast out the spirit, Jesus told them because of their "unbelief." He then added, "This kind goeth not out but by prayer and fasting" (Matt. 17:21).

The discussion among theologians is: "What did Christ mean by the statement 'this kind'?" Was He referring to this kind of *unbelief*, meaning there are different levels of unbelief and this type of unbelief in their hearts would only be removed by both prayer and fasting? From my experience, the only way to defeat unbelief is to overcome it through prayer and fasting, as this duel weapon raises your faith level. The second and more plausible theory is this type of spirit can only be cast out through prayer and fasting.

This narrative reveals that some spirits have more *strength* than others and are also more *stubborn* than others. All twelve disciples had previously been given delegated authority over all forms of spirits and diseases. *Yet, their faith was not equal to their authority.* I compare this fact to a believer who has a beautiful Bible with a leather cover, fine paper, gilded with gold on the outer edge, with two blue ribbon markers sitting on the bed stand, believing that the sight of the Bible will run off any evil spirit attempting to enter the premises. However, it is not a Torah Scroll or a physical Bible in and of itself that will frighten demons or serve like a hedge to prevent some unexpected encounter in your house. The words of the Bible must come off the pages and into your heart, where they can be spoken out of your mouth. If you have authority over the enemy, you must first believe you have authority before attempting to exercise that authority.

If parents have two children, usually one is compliant and the other is defiant. One will submit to instruction and the other will always challenge that authority. Demonic spirits are on different levels of authority. For some reason, some are weaker and others are stronger. The weaker are easier to expel and often control a person with a more passive personality. The bolder, more stubborn spirits are attracted to a more stubborn personality.

SOME SPIRITS ARE MORE WICKED

In a unique revelation, Christ taught that an unclean spirit will at times team up with other spirits "more wicked" than Himself (Luke 11:26). There are two Greek words translated as "wicked" in our English translation. One means to be lawless or by implication a criminal (2 Pet. 2:7; 3:17). The word used by Peter in 2 Peter 2:7 alludes to the men of Sodom who were not only immoral but also violent and lawless in their nature toward strangers in the city (see Gen. 19). Christ spoke of spirits "more wicked" than others. The Greek word for wicked here is *poneros,* and in this context refers to someone who is evil and immoral in character and in actions.

Christians often hear it stated that "all sins are the same." The word *sin* referring to the transgression of God's laws and statutes, and *sin* from the scriptural perspective, covers a broad meaning of acts of disobedience or immoral actions. However, people often place sin in different levels—small sins and big sins. Someone who willfully steals from another is not perceived by people in the same category as a man who rapes a woman. A person who tells a lie is not perceived by people on the same sin level as the person who practices idolatry, worshipping a false God. It must, however, be pointed out that the final destination of all unrepentant sinners is the same, the lake of fire, as "liars" and "idolaters" are listed in the same category as "murderers" and "whoremongers" (Rev. 21:8).

The *spiritual force* motivating the sin act is where there is often a difference. A person may be tempted to lie to cover for themselves or steal because they are greedy, but a demonic spirit may not necessarily be behind the basic motivation, as the inner Adamic sin nature often pushes men to yield to temptation and at times the human spirit is willing to do right but the flesh is weak (Mark 14:38).

We read in 2 Chronicles 18 of a "lying spirit" that deceived Ahab's four hundred prophets into prophesying false information to the king (1 Kings 22:22-23), leading to his death on the battlefield. At the same time Isaac told a lie, saying that his wife, Rebekah, was his sister, out of fear that King Abimelech's men would kill him and take Rebekah into the king's haram (Gen. 26:7). Ahab's prophets were inspired by a spirit but Isaac's lie was from his own choice. A perpetual liar who seems to never tell the truth can be under the spell of a lying spirit. Someone who tells a single lie is lying, but not necessarily under the influence of a "lying spirit." Achan, a soldier who entered Jericho, secretly stole certain valuable items, hiding them in his tent, ignoring divine instruction from Joshua that all of Jericho's spoils belonged to the treasury of the Lord. Achan stole by *choice* and not because he was controlled by an evil spirit (see Josh. 7). He confessed to Joshua that he "coveted" the silver and gold (Josh. 7:21); thus, he broke one of the Ten Commandments: "Thou shalt not covet." In the case of Job, when two different nomadic tribes invaded his property, stealing his oxen, donkeys, and camels, carrying them off into the deserts of Arabia, the motivation to steal from Job was initiated by Satan himself, who formed a strategy to destroy Job, hoping to discourage him and make him turn from God (see Job 1 and 2). In some instances spirits are involved and in other instance it is carnal choice.

What makes some spirits more wicked than others may be the *types of sin* they motivate people to do. One of my closest friends once worked for the military on a classified level. I asked her what was the one thing she learned that was the most disturbing. She said, "How totally inhumane and wicked a human being can be toward another human, such as when terrorists murder children and how they torture people without any consideration of the pain the person is experiencing." There is no doubt that terror organizations such as ISIS are motivated by a level of demon spirits that are more wicked than other spirits, as ISIS will behead innocent people, rape young girls, burn men alive in cages, and preform acts of abuse and torture that are beyond comprehension. The more heinous the sin, the more wicked the spirit.

Wicked spirits seem to move in groups of sevens. Christ taught that a weaker spirit will "take seven other spirits more wicked," enter a person, and dwell in them. Christ cast seven devils out of Mary Magdalene (Luke 8:2). Mary Magdalene was a sinner whom Christ delivered from demons, who remained free throughout her life as she wholly served the Lord. In Luke's reference, the seven other more wicked are spirits that return to a person who was temporarily clean (the "house" swept and garnished), but the person opens a door for the enemy to return (some scholars suggest this is the condition of a backslider—one who knew Christ but willfully returns to sin). Once these seven spirits possess the person, their spiritual, moral, and mental condition is worse than their original condition. Spirits of sexual or moral *perversion* are a prime example. The word *perverse* is found twenty times in the English translation of the Bible, with a wide variety of meanings, including to be *rash* (Num. 22:32); to be *distorted and crooked* (Deut. 32:5); to *commit iniquity and wrong* (1 Sam. 20:30); of *coveting* (Job 6:30) and so forth. Jesus was so frustrated with the unbelief and hypocrisy of His generation, He called them a "faithless and perverse generation" (Luke 9:41). An individual that is perverse in their mind or spirit has become crooked or twisted in their thinking, which leads to deception and lies. A perverse individual may look clean on the outside, but the inner heart and spirit is filthy and corrupt.

The most common spirit of perversion is linked with sexual addiction through pornography. Research has been conducted on how pornography impacts the mind and why there is great harm and danger in pornographic addiction. The eyes transfer the visual to the mind, which records the image on the brain. Over time the pictures are not enough to quench the desire for more, leading to video or computer addiction. Over time the videos are not enough and a person finds themselves sneaking to strip clubs. After seeing the "live" acts, eventually prostitution enters the picture. Eventually if a man is married, he will often divorce his wife to live in a fantasy world.

At some point during the addiction, a more *wicked spirit* moves into the heart of the person, controlling them and pushing them into a deeper bondage. Despite the level of authority of influence a spirit has over a person, deliverance from all types of spirits can be found through Christ.

THE FIRST REQUIREMENT FOR FREEDOM

The first requirement to exercise dominion over evil and unclean spirits is to receive a redemptive covenant and personal relationship with the Lord Jesus Christ. This covenant purges us from sin and assists in controlling the sin nature. The power of a covenant relationship (or lack thereof) was evident when seven Jewish men, sons of Sceva, a priest living in Ephesus (Acts 19:13-14), who claimed to be "exorcists," took it upon themselves to expel a strong evil spirit from a man. They were called "vagabond Jews" (Acts 19:13). The word *vagabond* in Greek means "to circle around" or "to wander around." These men were wandering throughout the town looking for some spiritual action. These seven had the "religious training," but not the personal relationship with Christ. They used a verbal formula saying, "We command you by Jesus whom Paul preaches to come of this man" (Acts 19:13). The demon spoke, confessing that he knew both Jesus and Paul, but had no idea who these men were. Instead of the demonic spirit coming out of the man, the seven men were observed running out of the man's house stripped, naked and embarrassed, when the possessed man went into a rage and attacked them. This was a strong, stubborn spirit that physically attacked seven unprepared men. They had a "formula" without a "foundation." The foundation of your faith is not your head knowledge of spiritual facts but in your personal prayer life and intimate fellowship with Jesus Christ. This relationship is entered into through repentance of sins and receiving Christ as Lord and Savior. Once you have secured an active, talking, and fellowshipping relationship with Christ, this connection leads to the next requirement.

THE SECOND REQUIREMENT

You must have an understanding of your *spiritual authority* in Christ. The word *authority* used in the New Testament is a necessary requirement needed to cast out devils (Mark 1:27). The same Greek word for "authority" is used when alluding to Jesus' power over *devils* (Mark 1:27), the authority to *preach* (Matt. 7:29), and His authority to execute *judgment* (John 5:27). This Greek word for "authority" in these narratives is *exousia*, which is a privilege or right transferred from one who has authority to another who receives that authority from the giver. For example, I can ride in a police car at night and people think I must be a police officer. However, if an arrest is made, I cannot become involved as I am not an officer of the law—but just a guy riding with an officer. Just because you attend a church, does not instantly give you an authority license. Riding in a police car doesn't make me the sheriff, and attending a church doesn't give me special authority.

My best example of exercising authority comes from my early revivals. I recall two specific instances, when individuals who were completely possessed by spirits responded to an alar invitation. At age eighteen in Roanoke, Virginia, while I was ministering to people during the altar service, a strong spirit began manifesting. Immediately some church members discerned the spirit and began praying for the person's deliverance, while I saw other "altar workers" like cowards backing away in fear. One hour before this incident, if I were to ask both groups—those later casting out the spirit and those hiding near the metal folding chairs—"Do you believe you have authority over all devils?" these Pentecostals would have all shouted, "Yes!" However, it was evident that a few believed they could expel this spirit and some didn't have the faith, or were afraid of the challenge.

Authority cannot be released in silence. Authority manifests as God backs up your prayers and preaching. Authority is delegated, or legally handed down from a giver to a receiver. In a believer's case it is the power to act on behalf of another, using their name and their high position. In the secular world lawyers call this transfer the "power of attorney"—when one person legally transfers the rights for another person to sign legal documents or speak on their behalf. For example, because my wife and I are married and in a legal bond called a marital covenant, at our marriage she dropped her last name, Taylor, and took my last name, Stone. She can sign checks, pay bills, and do all forms of business because of our legal covenant relationship. Christ knew He would return to heaven as our heavenly (priestly) representative, yet also understood that His future spiritual family, in covenant with Him, would live on a planet under the spiritual, moral, and political influence of Satan's dark kingdom. By defeating death, hell, the grave, and Satan, Christ transferred His legal, delegated authority over "all of the powers of the enemy" to us (Luke 10:19).

It is important to note that all spirits connected to Satan can detect if a person is in a true relationship with Christ and if they have true spiritual authority. When a person knows their position and relationship in God's kingdom, they can pray with power, authority, and confidence. When a person questions their relationship with Christ or is uncertain of their authority, this uncertainty can be detected and capitalized upon by even the weakest of evil spirits, which is what occurred when the disciples could not cast out an epileptic spirit. This spirit sensed their unbelief, and no evil spirit is required to listen to a rebuke to depart from the mouth of a believer whose heart that is wrapped in unbelief. Spirits can sense both faith and unbelief. When unbelief is present, it prevents the spirit from departing (see Matt. 17:14-20).

The presence of strong unbelief creates an atmosphere. This is why on occasions, when Christ would pray, He would remove everyone from the room, to prevent this spirit of unbelief from hindering His prayers. In one case, a young girl died and Christ told them she was not dead but sleeping. The crowd in the house began mocking Him. He removed everyone from the room except the mother and father and raised the child from the dead (Mark 5:39-41). In Nazareth, Christ could not perform any great miracles "because of their unbelief" (Matt. 13:58). I have ministered in churches where I would teach and share amazing stories of modern miracles, only to sense a resistance emerging from some in the audience. Unbelief creates a negative charge in the atmosphere and actually suppresses faith from activating, when doubt is strong. In such an atmosphere, praying for people feels like you are laying your hands on a cold, brass doorknob or on a sheet rock wall. If I and other believers can sense such a level of unbelief, then the entire spirit world can.

Once spiritual authority is established in your mind, heart, and spirit, the next important ingredient to exercising power of evil spirits is to have a complete revelation on the power the name of Jesus Christ has over every spirit of darkness. Your authority over Satan is not contingent upon how long you have been a church member, or how many years ago you were converted. Your victory lies in the finished and completed atoning work Christ completed on the cross and the defeat Satan encountered at His resurrection. It was Christ who said, "All power (authority) is given me both in heaven and in earth." Paul revealed that at the name of Jesus all things in heaven, in earth, and under the earth must bow and confess He is Lord (Phil. 2:10-11).

REQUIREMENT NUMBER THREE

The third requirement when expelling demons is to have faith in the authority vested in the name of Jesus. There is a debate within the Body of Christ as to the translation of the name of Jesus we should use when praying to the heavenly Father. Some suggest that the English translation from the Greek of the name of *Jesus* is not the proper name to use when we pray. Since Christ was a Hebrew and not a Greek, we should be praying using His name in Hebrew, which is Yeshua, and not the name Jesus, which is translated from the Greek.

First it should be noted that in Christ's day there were four major languages known and spoken in Israel. The Greeks used Greek, the Romans used Latin, and the devout Jews used Hebrew, while many living in the Galilee spoke a Syriac-Aramaic. In the Galilean synagogues, the Scriptures were read using the Septuagint translation, which is the Old Testament translated from Hebrew to Greek. Jews from a variety of nations were present on Passover, observing the inscription that Pilate etched on a wooden board on the cross that read, "Jesus of Nazareth the King of the Jews" (John 19:19). It was written in Hebrew, Greek, and Latin so that those who spoke these three languages would understand the saying (John 19:20).

Consider the following. Some of Christ's followers called Him *Rabbi*, others addressed Him as *Lord*, and still others, such as Peter, called Him the *Christ*—which means "the anointed one." As rabbi, He was the greatest teacher; as Lord, He is the owner of all things; as Jesus, He was the prophet sent to man; and as Christ, He was the promised Messiah. Without spending pages in a debate, the fact is that when missionaries from the United States—who speak English—travel to any foreign nation in the world, which requires a person to translate from English to the language of that particular nation, when they speak the name "Jesus," all evil and unclean spirits in every nation recognize Christ's name! For hundreds of years, missionaries from England and America have spread the Gospel net among the African tribes to the Arabs in the Middle East, and millions have been won to Christ after praying a salvation prayer "in the name of Jesus!"

If we are commanding the enemy to leave and we do not have faith in the power of his name, then we are not exercising our covenant authority given to us to use His name. Christ said, "I my name you shall cast out devils" (Mark 16:17). Christ instructed His disciples to go forth and cast out devils using His name. When they returned they replied, "Even the devils are subject unto us through thy name" (Luke 10:17-19).

GET FREE AND STAY FREE

Jesus healed a man and said, "Go and sin no more lest a worst thing come upon you" (John 5:14). When an unnamed woman was forgiven of adultery, Jesus said, "Go and sin no more" (John 8:11). John wrote that "He whom the son sets free is free indeed" (John 8:36). The Greek word here for "free" not only refers to being completely liberated, but to be exempt from any ceremonial of moral liability. This is important due to the previous event that occurred when Christ spoke this. He had just forgiven a woman caught in adultery who according to Moses' law should have been stoned for her sin (Lev. 20:10). Christ in the same setting says that whom He frees is free indeed, and the word *free* (*indeed*) also means to free someone from moral liability or ceremonial liability. He released her from her sin and from the act of stoning. Thus, she was free indeed!

The challenge for a person whom Christ has freed is to maintain that freedom without turning back to a lifestyle of sin—to "sin no more" so that nothing worse can come upon them. When Jesus spoke of the unclean spirit leaving a newly cleaned house, He said the spirit that departed will take seven others more wicked and make an attempt to return. If they can succeed, then the condition of the person is worse than previous. Each person who has been truly delivered must understand that there will be a counterattack at some point planned by the same spirits that originally held you captive. However, they do not have to be successful, as Christ has given you power (authority) over all of the powers of the enemy (Luke 10:18-19).

Authority Is the Key

My Father, Fred Stone, once preached a powerful message in which he identified Christ as "The Devil Stalker," meaning that if Christ discerned anyone was being manipulated, oppressed, or possessed by a spirit, He would set out to seek their freedom and deliverance. Jesus and demons can't stay in the same room together! When Christ dealt with the man in the synagogue, demanding the evil spirit come out, when the fellow was delivered the entire congregation was amazed and said, ". . . For with authority he commands even the unclean spirits" (Mark 1:17).

During Christ's ministry, there were times when He asked the spirit what was its name (Mark 5:9), and at other times He refused to even allow the spirit to speak, by commanding, "Hold your peace" (Luke 4:35). One reason for forbidding a spirit to speak was often the demon publicly recognized Christ, calling Him the "Son of God." This public recognition was misread by the Pharisees, who initiated a whispering campaign among the multitudes that since the devils knew Jesus, then he must be in some form of a secret pact or agreement with them, through Beelzebub the chief demon (Mark 3:22). Christ knew He was God's son and needed no confirmation from the kingdom of darkness to authenticate He and God's relationship.

Notice that in no instance did Christ carry on some long, dramatic conversation with any spirit. Since Satan is the Father of lies (John 8:44), then his posse of spirits carries Satan's lying nature. Any extended conversation with demonic entities, to gain some type of "unknown spiritual insight," would more likely lead to a distortion, a deception, or an overly dramatic manifestation to draw attention to themselves. During my many years of ministry I have occasionally been in services where believers were attempting to expel an unclean spirit from a person. On one occasion, the man directing the "exorcism" was more interested in attempting to discover some mysterious knowledge of the spirit world than he was seeing the person delivered. I realized this spirit was entertaining the people and drawing undue attention to itself. These types of alleged "exorcisms" can go on for what seems to be an eternity, until finally the people praying the prayers for deliverance are worn out, the person seeing help is practically asleep, and the director of the deliverance has a notebook, of strange notes, that some lying spirit spoke that were recorded as amazing facts. Christ should be our example, that when a person controlled by a spirit seeks help, there should be a strong, firm command using our faith, and Christ's delegated authority should be with power, authority for the spirit to leave immediately. When Jesus would say, "Come out," there was no argument and no resistance, as no demonic adversary can resist Christ's authority.

Timing a Deliverance

There is also a timing element involved when dealing with certain types of spirits. In the New Testament, Christ and the Apostles would respond *once a spirit began manifesting* in a person. Notice Paul's delayed reaction when dealing with a fortune teller in Philippi:

> *"Now it happened, as we went to prayer, that a certain slave girl possessed with a spirit of divination met us, who brought her masters much profit by fortune-telling. This girl followed Paul and us, and cried out, saying, "These men are the servants of the Most High God, who proclaim to us the way of salvation. And this she did for many days. But Paul, greatly annoyed, turned and said to the spirit, "I command you in the name of Jesus Christ to come out of her. And he came out that very hour."*
> —Acts 16:16-18 (NKJV)

The twist to this story is that the spirit within the woman was saying, "These are servants of the Most-High God," which was a true statement. When unclean spirits recognized Christ as "The Son of God," this was also a fact. However, the enemy will *acknowledge a truth* if by accepting it the person is later pulled into a trap of eventual deception. All heretical beliefs that emerged in the first four centuries of the church did not originate with a false teaching, but a teacher began with truth that was later distorted or perverted, leading to spiritual deception. This woman's words were true but her psychic occupation and the spirit of divination working through her was demonic. It is possible that the spirit possessing her desired not to be exposed and cast out, and therefore hid under a true statement, thinking Paul would not respond to her.

Notice that she went before them for "many days." Observe that Paul was becoming agitated or annoyed, to the point that he could no longer permit a demon-possessed woman being his front-person announcing his ministry. Paul's *timing* of this deliverance was triggered by his spiritual uneasiness and agitation, stirring his spirit to action. This same spiritual agitation was witnessed at the tomb of Lazarus. As Christ prepared to raise His friend from the dead, those surrounding the tomb were filled with unbelief. We read that Jesus "groaned in his spirit and was troubled" (John 11:33). The Greek word for "groaned" is from a root word meaning "to snort in anger," or to "sigh heavily." Jesus was "troubled;" the Greek word here being *tarasso*, meaning "to stir or agitate." The imagery is water that is rolling and being tossed around. The people's unbelief was agitating Christ as He groaned "in the spirit" (John 11:33). When a Holy Spirit-baptized believer confronts a person controlled by evil spirits, there is an uneasiness or agitation the believer can discern in their own spirit. This is a clash of spirits—one filled with light and the other with darkness.

THE CLASH OF WILLS

There is a God-given human capacity called the human "will," in which an individual intentionally chooses to commit an act or to avoid the situation. From the creation of Adam in the garden, God gave mankind a choice between life and death, good and evil. When Israel evolved into God's chosen nation, He revealed His written law through Moses, saying for Israel to "choose" (Deut. 7:7; 30:19), meaning to make a selection or a decision, usually between two opposites, or between multiple choices. Often, what makes a person decide or choose one thing over the other is the benefits acquired by making a particular choice. When certain benefits are detected in the reward part of the brain, the brain will send positive signals to the rest of the body to move toward the reward. Good and bad choices can be made, depending upon the desire to be rewarded, including some form of pleasure that tickles the five senses. Drugs, alcohol, and pornography release specific chemicals in the brain, such as dopamine and serotonin, which stimulate the reward centers in the brain, thus motivating a person to choose improperly something that could be damaging later, in order to experience a momentary, brief feeling of pleasure.

A believer must submit their will, to the will of God, to enter the New Covenant and to enjoy the numerous spiritual benefits provided through the atoning work of Christ. When a sinner or a backslider has become demonized and under the influence or control of unclean or evil spirits, there must be a willingness of the person to submit to prayer and the opportunity for total deliverance. When Christ stepped off the boat, the possessed man from the tombs came running toward Him (Mark 5:5). Some suggest the demons were motivating the man to attack Christ and do Him harm. However, once the demons clashed with presence of Christ, the man fell to the ground and the evil spirits were now under subjection to the will and authority of Christ. The main point is, if you are willing to submit your mind, spirit, and body to Christ and to the Holy Spirit, it is impossible for the powers of Satan—in any form—to hold on to you.

That night in Tennessee when I offered a prayer of deliverance to a girl who chose to remain in her sins, there were eyewitnesses who were upset with me because I stopped praying. I tried to explain a very important principle. First, God does not and will not overpower anyone's will and force Himself upon them. If overriding man's will were God's method of reaching the lost, He could force His will upon every living human into serving Him, as it is not His will that any perish (2 Pet. 3:9). This girl chose darkness over God's light, and neither God nor myself could or would overpower her desire to remain in her perverse lifestyle. Second, the Bible teaches that if an individual spirit is released from a person, and roams for a brief period, it will return, bringing more wicked spirits with him, and re-enter the former victim, causing the person's condition to worsen (see Matt. 11:42-45). If I would have been successful in expelling this spirit from the girl, and she would have returned back to her sin (which she did), opening a door for more wicked spirits to enter her, increasing their stronghold in her.

One way a former demonized victim can maintain their deliverance and close the door on unwanted spirits is to testify to others of what God has done. After the man of Gedera was completely freed, Christ told him to return home and tell his friends of the great things the Lord had done for him (Mark 5:19). Christ was confirming what John later penned in Revelation, that believers overcome Satan by the "blood of the lamb and the word of their testimony" (Rev. 12:11).

We have in our OCI youth ministry numerous youth whom at age eleven saw pornography on their phones or on the internet and became addicted. In each case these kids began to cry out to the Lord and were free from this bondage. They also began to attend church and fellowship with other youth who were on fire for God. They will often give a public testimony, which not only helps others but helps to hold them to accountability that God has freed them and they should not return to their former mental prison.

When an individual seeks deliverance from demonic oppression, depression, or possession, they must be willing to submit their whole being—body, soul, and spirit—to the will of God and not resist the prayer and the ministry it requires to bring them freedom.

10 | LIFE LESSONS I HAVE LEARNED FROM SPIRITUAL WARFARE

There are three significant methods of learning—experience, experience, and experience! Perhaps you thought I would suggest the process—elementary school, high school, and college. Secular teachers set goals of teaching history, English, math, and other subjects required to successfully live in a contemporary society. However, all the book reading, tests, and discussions will be meaningless until the classroom information can be tested and proven in life situations. One of my close friends graduated with a bachelor's degree in pastoring and was ready to enter full-time ministry, putting into practice all he learned. His first church had eight members, and the sanctuary was tiny, mildewed, and falling apart. The parsonage (home) he would live in had holes in the ceiling and rotting wooden floors. The church membership had split; the remaining members were old, tired, and restless. After a few months he told me, "I have to just about 'throw out' many of my college professor's theories I learned in school, because they didn't include how to deal with frustrated members who are continually in conflict."

Consider this: all theology is based upon the encounters and experiences of men and women of God in Scriptures. There were angels on assignment before Angelology was ever taught. There were strategies and assignments of evil and unclean spirits, long before the first Bible College course Demonology 101 was offered. The visions or at times dreams of Daniel and the Apostle John in Revelation are called Apocalyptic literature—a term used for something hidden that is made known or revealed. Prophetic teaching is based upon the visions of prophets that revealed the future. The doctrine of Soteriology (salvation) and Pneumatology (the Holy Spirit) would never exist, had it not been for the act of Christ's redemption and the ministry of the Holy Spirit. All biblical doctrine was formulated out of the dynamic spiritual experiences of holy men and women of God.

True knowledge is what authenticates and confirms our spiritual experiences. If an experience contradicts the revelation within Scripture, it is a man-induced or a false spirit teaching. Thus, experience is where we gain most of our life-experience knowledge but knowledge must also be gained from others, chiefly the revelation penned in the Scripture. During my numerous years of biblical study, life experience, and personal spiritual encounters, I have gained valuable points of insight that I believe will be an asset to the reader.

Lesson 1—Demons Don't Age but You Do

Consider the following: our generation is battling the same fallen angel *Satan* that deceived Adam and Eve (Gen. 3), set an assignment against Job (Job 1 and 2), resisted the rebuilding of the Temple in Jerusalem (Zech. 3:1-3), tempted Jesus for forty days (Matt. 4:1-6), and hindered Paul throughout his ministry (2 Cor. 12:7). We are battling the same *demons* that have existed since human government was formed. During six thousand years these malicious spirits have known every human flaw, character weakness, spiritual trap door, and any effective weapons that can be used to bring destruction and death. These spirits have one major advantage—and it's not just their knowledge. It is their longevity. *They never get old and die, but humans do.*

Their age has no bearing on their ability, but our strength weakens with our age. When David was a teenager he *ran* to the giant Goliath, but later in his life another giant with a new sword almost killed him (1 Sam. 17:48; 2 Sam. 21:16). Peter, a brash fisherman, fished all night and cleaned nets in the morning, requested to walk on water, and secretly followed Jesus to His night trial. He was mobile and agile and always on the move. However, after Christ's resurrection the Messiah informed him that in his *old age* he would require the assistance of others and be carried places (John 21:18). Only one man in the Bible seemed to have had an edge on the secrets of the "fountain of youth" and that was Moses. When reaching 120 years of age, his eyesight was not dim and neither were his natural forces abated (Deut. 34:7). Extended periods of fasting can renew your body, and in Moses' case he experienced two back-to-back forty-day fasts, totaling eighty days without food (Exod. 24:18; 34:28). Obviously, *God's presence sustained him and made him younger in body than in age!*

After many years of ministry, I am wise enough to know that I can't fight with the same boundless zeal and energy that I did when I was in my twenties. My spirit still burns with zeal my mind is sharp but my body becomes tired easier. David even confessed this when he wrote:

"And I am weak today, though anointed king; and these men, the sons of Zeruiah, are too harsh for me. The LORD shall repay the evildoer according to his wickedness."
—2 Samuel 3:39

In the context of this verse, the writer speaks of the long war that occurred between the house of David and the house of Saul (2 Sam. 3:1). David lived many years on the run, like a hunted animal, hiding in caves and elusive mountain fortresses, surrounded by six hundred men protecting his future destiny. Saul had given David's wife to another man, and Saul attempted to manipulate his own son, Jonathan, to turn against this young warrior. David eventually became so weary from the battle that he crossed the Judean border, leaving the security of his tribal land grant in Judah to live with his enemies—the Philistines. In David's later years, he remained at his palace in

Jerusalem during war cycles when kings went to battle.

Your mind can become "foggy" with age. This doesn't sound exciting but it is true. As a person becomes older, their mind can become slightly dull. Older people comment, "Now where did I put those keys?" and "Who took my money?" (which you later find in the other pair of pants). How many times have older adults said, "Now what was I going to say?" Just remember, the enemy has no compassion and no exemption clauses in your retirement package. He will never let you slide into home plate without resistance. Satan will never say, "Well, let's leave sister Shundi and brother Hallie alone because they just don't have the strength to fight us anymore!" Satan's trophies include all ages throughout the ages who have fallen in the battle, stopped running the race, or lost by default.

Christ Himself became tired after long hours of face-to-face ministry, forcing Him to separate from the masses and resort into a desert area for rest and quiet (Matt. 14:30). Paul wrote:

"For consider him that endured such contradiction of sinners against himself, lest ye be wearied and faint in your minds."
—Hebrews 12:3

Never believe that if you live long you must do so with only half of your mind and a third of your body. My Granddad Bava, who passed at age eighty-six, and my grandmother, who passed at age eighty-four, maintained clear and alert minds up to the day before they passed from this life, still recalling details of years past with amazing accuracy.

Your spirit will remain strong with age. There is some good news as we talk about an older body and foggy thinking. Once your spirit has filled up your adult body, your inner man or inner spirit man will never age the way your body ages. At death your body will return to the dust and your spirit to God, who gave it (Eccl. 12:7). We can remain "mighty in spirit" and "strong in spirit." Paul wrote:

"That he would grant you, according to the riches of his glory, to be strengthened with might by his Spirit in the inner man."
— Ephesians 3:16

We must always fight with the energy of our spirit more than the strength of our body or the reflections in our mind. Our warfare is called a "spiritual" war, meaning the conflict is centered upon the eternal spirit of a person—the spirit that will live on for eternity after it exits the body where it was once housed.

LESSON 2—TEMPTATION NEVER ENDS—IT JUST CHANGES SEASONS

Your life, including your spiritual life, moves through cycles and seasons. Notice what occurs during the three stages of life. In our *youthful* years as a single young adult we are instructed in Scripture to "flee youthful lusts" (2 Tim. 2:22). This would indicate self-control involving the human sex drive, which is powerful in the late teen and early twenties, especially with young men. Some youth unleash their passion and awaken love before the proper time, believing that everyone they kiss and grip in their affection is the one they are truly in love with. Instead of love they are recycling lustful passions. As most people approach their *twenties*, they usually find their soul mate, making plans to marry. After engagement and prior to marriage the pressure to just "do it anyway" can mount, causing a burning temptation. Paul wrote that it is better to "Marry than to burn" (1 Cor. 7:9). In the Scriptural context, this does not refer to burning in hell because of some sin, but burning with a "hot" desire for that so-called "hot" future companion. Thus, it is better to marry and enter a legal marital covenant than for a couple to burn continually for one another and fall into continual fornication.

As a rather personal and funny note, in February 1980, I met a nineteen-year old girl named Pam Taylor who flipped my world upside down—just looking at her! At age twenty, I was so consumed with ministry that I had thought, "Maybe I will just remain single for a long time and dedicate myself wholly to the call of God." After all, during those early years I spent up to ten hours a day in study and prayer mixed with fasting, and was quite content to be by myself with no distractions. I assure you my intentions were pure and my heart was sincerely focused on God and God alone. However, once I began talking to Pam, calling her on the phone and from time to time getting to be with her, I knew I was not called to the life of a Protestant monk and had no desire to hug pillows the rest of my life. Just the thought of a honeymoon with her caused me to speed up my proposal after two years of long-distance "phone dating" (I continually traveled). With her and Jesus I knew we could do anything as a team!

Some youth may believe that once they are married with a companion of their "dreams" that temptation toward the opposite sex will end and that battle is forever won. Sadly, this is not the case, as the Adamic flesh nature is still attached to our physical bodies, and at times an un-renewed mind will take its own journey to places it shouldn't. This fact can be seen with the number of marriages that have fallen apart or ended in a divorce because of a husband or wife departing from their companion for another person. For some that fire of "burning" love that was the super-glue that would do in an early relationship dies out in the ashes of separation, and another "fire" begins burning in another person's field.

Once *married*, a husband and wife must learn to walk a balance of spiritual and marital commitments. Paul spoke of a husband and wife spending time separated from sexual intimacy during set seasons of prayer and fasting, and warned both to come together again, in their physical relations, lest Satan tempt them for being inconsistent in this area (1 Cor. 7:5). If one marital partner is willfully or by choice not meeting the *physical marital needs* of the other, they are biblically in error and hold a key that could open the door to Satan tempting their companion with the opposite sex. A husband or wife who desires intimacy or affection and is ignored can at times turn to others to vent their frustrations, which leads to a temptation in their flesh.

One danger is when a married person begins to rekindle a "flame" from the past through social media, such as Facebook. I have known of five different cases in which a woman left her husband for a former boyfriend she had in high school or college.

For the average Christian couple, as a woman ages, the more she enjoys and appreciates family time and alone time with her husband. As a husband ages, he often desires more affection from his wife, especially since the wife is often a mom who has split her attention and affection with children for many years!

One of the activities my wife and I have tried to focus on is to set aside time for just me and her—without the kids (and their friends) and without cares. From time to time I have a free weekend and she will book a hotel out of town and we just get away for a mini-honeymoon. I actually have a special car I call my "date car" that we take on these trips to Alabama football games. Honestly, I don't like the new cars, because they have a divider between the two front seats and she can't sit close to me like she did in the early days of the one seat front seats.

Remember, temptation will always be present in some form; perhaps not in the same forms as in the past, but the seasons in life will introduce different and new challenges, until the day we depart this life.

LESSON 3—CHANGING SEASONS MEANS CHANGING SPIRITS

The planning and strategies of any natural war changes as situations change. American soldiers do not fight with the same strategies in an *open desert* such as Iraq as they do in the *rugged mountains* of Afghanistan. While the weapons remain the same, the difficulty of the operation and timing of attacks must be considered. Because of the sudden sandstorms, rain seasons, cold mountain winters with snow, and the shifting of the winds, new challenges are faced.

For example, the timing of the Gulf War (1991) was in the winter and not the hot summer. One reasons was the direction of the wind currents that must be considered, as many believe Saddam Hussein was concealing chemical weapons and could tip a missile, sending it into Arabia where U.S. bases were positioned. It would have been best if the wind blew in an *opposite direction* of where our troops were stationed. Heavy rain can be hazardous for heavy equipment (especially with mud), and in mountainous regions water flowing off mountains can suddenly flood a road or bridge within minutes. In Israel, during the winter, a sudden flash storm can occur, sending water down the slopes of the Judean Wilderness into the dry riverbeds, filling them so fast that, at times, buses and vehicles have been caught on a water-covered road, unable to pass. These floods never occur during the hot summer, but when the season changes to winter the atmosphere shifts as the dry air is replaced with moisture and clouds.

In life, your seasons will change (Eccl. 3:1). You may have been a picture of health at age twenty-five, but at age fifty-five you are battling a hereditary disease. In your early marriage you may have been in love like Romeo and Juliet, but in your forties the cares of life are snuffing out the flame of love. You may have worked for one company for thirty years and find yourself laid off in a concealed merger—needing now to learn how to use modern technology at age fifty. Then there are the numerous battles with rebellious children, addictions, and a list of weapons of destruction.

In my teen years I battled a terrible feeling of insecurity, leading to depression. After this season, my ministry was attacked with false information from hateful people that took a long time to correct. At times messages I preached were misunderstood, causing some within my ministry denomination to consider my Hebraic roots teaching as heresy, and I was maligned by some who didn't understand this "Old Testament teaching." It seemed that when one conflict was settled, a new one was just over the horizon. In retrospect, I believe these were well designed strategies to wear me down emotionally, mentally, and spiritually. However, I have a strong will and some Italian blood in me that can boil occasionally, motivating me to head into the fight instead of taking flight!

When you enter new seasons, you may battle new spirits. David killed Goliath in one season but was faced with Lahmi, Goliath's brother in a later season (2 Chron.

20:5). The same God that helped David slay a giant as a teenager helped him defeat Goliath's brother in his older age. Different types of spirits may come, but the Word of the Lord changes not.

These trials forced me into a dependency upon the Lord. God will never break when you lean on Him! He loves for you to say, "I need you," and the same faith that brought your first deliverance will continue to keep you delivered.

LESSON 4—LEARN TO WIN THE WARS OTHERS HAVE LOST

For years I have made this statement: *"The greatest lesson you will ever learn is to learn your lesson the first time."* In ministry, one of the greatest mysteries is how a person can experience freedom and yet over time repeat the same cycle of bondage over and over again, as though they never learned from their past experiences. If I walked every day through a neighborhood with a huge dog that was waiting to attack me, I would avoid that road and find a different path. If there was a bully on the playground that knocked me down every day, I would either learn how to whip him or play in another playground. I am not saying to run from your adversity, but do not be willing offer yourself upon the altar of abuse in the name of being persecuted for God's sake. At times we are assigned a battle with the goal of defeating a foe, but at other times the foe is not fighting but hoping you will enter his domain where he can take advantage of you. You must quit visiting the old battlefields of the past, and reliving memories of old wounds.

My Father, Fred Stone was a pack-rat when it came to religious articles written by anyone knowledgeable or versed in Scripture. From his youth until he was in his fifties, he collected articles and magazines and filled file cabinets with biblical sermons, from Baptist, Methodist, and Pentecostal ministers. When I was a teenage minister, I discovered that Dad had numerous articles dating back to the days of what was termed "The Healing Revival." The sermons came from noted tent evangelists who in their day ministered to thousands each night in cities across America.

Several of these men, in their later years, battled terrible weakness in their flesh and two in particular had become entangled in the use of alcohol, causing one to become a full-blown alcoholic. In one instance, a noted tent minister purchased a tent twelve inches larger than America's leading tent evangelist, allowing him to announce that he was the proud owner of the "World's largest Gospel tent," which manifest obvious pride instead of humility. Several of these men who paid a high price in fasting and prayer ministered twice a day for weeks on end, only to discover that when the anointing lifted and their hectic schedule concluded, they were "burnt out," struggling to regain strength. Some were forced out of the ministry. While it was not as common in the late 1940s and '50s, occasionally a married minister would "run off" with another woman. Some struggled to continue in ministry, and others dropped out of the race, falling short of the finish line.

During my last two years in high school, I poured over written testimonies and eyewitness accounts of miracles, while also learning lessons of what caused the downfall— the failures and defeats of men who were called, anointed, and appointed and yet, like Samson, gave way to a weakness in which they either could not or chose not to recover from. During those several years of study, I learned five lessons, in which I have tried to follow myself.

- Live a good, prosperous, yet modest life and place all *ministry income* back into the ministry
- Always give God all of the glory and never take glory to yourself for any accomplishment
- Stay in love with your wife, spending time with her and the kids—*don't get too busy for family*
- You are not superman and must *rest* or you can burn out and become an echo instead of a voice
- You can fall just like other men have—but learn from their past and *don't repeat their battle*

If you have a secret struggle, a character flaw, or some weakness in the soul, spirit or flesh, it would be wise to study the lives of those who too struggled in the same area and were able to obtain a deliverance or freedom from their weaknesses.

LESSON 5—THE HOLY SPIRIT HELPS OUR WEAKNESSES

I grew up in a very traditional Full-Gospel (Pentecostal) denomination. I have nothing at all negative to say about the wonderful godly people, the ministers, or the leadership, as their heart's desire was to lay aside anything of this world that would hinder their walk with God. This desire, however, went from beyond a *spiritual commitment* to an outward emphasis of avoiding makeup and avoiding jewelry. All women were required to wear a dress and never "pants." This caused a person's "spirituality" to be judged by what they *didn't* do and not what they *did* do.

The "right" outward appearance can often fake others out, as the right walk, look, and talk can appear holy, when the internal parts (the heart and mind) are in the wrong. I can recall church members and attendees being critically judged by others according to their outward appearance. At times the preaching was very judgmental and condemning and human failure was continually pointed out on a weekly basis. In reality, instead of making believers feel strong, I often felt weak and unworthy of any of God's blessing. I saw God not as a Father, but as a cosmic bully who really hated everyone, and no one could match up to his restrictions, but in order to "help you get free," He had a huge cosmic stick and would knock you down, thus forcing you to live His way. Honestly, I grew up and never comprehended how much God loved people—including those "wretched hell-bound sinners."

The fact is, most people do have a weakness of some form; a quick temper, seasons of depression, addictions, lust of the eyes or flesh, fear, doubt, unbelief—something, like a small tick clinging to an animal slowly sucking the blood out. In light of our weaknesses, here is a good Word from the Bible:

> *Likewise the Spirit also helpeth our infirmities . . ."*
> —Romans 8:26 (KJV)

The word *infirmities* in Greek is *astheneia*, which can refer to a moral, a spiritual, or even a physical weakness. The *physical weakness* can be infirmities of the flesh that attack the physical body, causing pain, weakness, or illness. In Luke 5:15, many people came to Christ to be "healed of their infirmities." A *mental infirmity* can be excess grief and sorrow that comes through a death, or manic depression, panic attacks, or excessive temptation. One spiritual weakness, according to Paul in Romans 8, is the lack of knowing *what* we should pray for as we should (Rom. 8:26). Since the Holy Spirit knows the mind and the will of God, He can help our weaknesses.

Spirits of infirmity must be exposed and either rebuked or cast out. In Luke 13, a daughter of Abraham (a Jewish woman, faithful to the Law of God) was attending a local synagogue when she encountered an unexpected deliverance service customized just for her. For eighteen years she walked bent over, unable to lift herself up straight. Luke indicates that the root source of her sickness was a "spirit of infirmity" (Luke 13:11)—or weakness. Any "weakness," whether mental, spiritual, or physical, will keep you bent over, unable to run the race and complete your assignments. Before Christ "laid his hands on her" (Luke 13:13), He "loosed her" from this infirm spirit (Luke 13:12). The Greek word for "loosed" here is *apoluo*, and alludes to fully freeing and sending something away. Christ freed the woman from the spirit and sent the spirit away from the woman. These types of spirits often seek to return to the former victim, and must be resisted. Perhaps this is why, when Christ exorcised a spirit from a young child, He commanded the spirit to "enter no more into him" (Mark 9:25).

This verbal command by Christ is often overlooked by those who pray for the demonic oppressed or possessed. Christ understood that when a spirit departs from the "house" it once possessed, it will seek at some point to return to the place from where it was expelled (see Luke 11:24-26). It is like someone who loses their home because they cannot make their payments, moves out their furniture (their goods), and the door closes behind them—yet they continue to fight the bank and mortgage company for access to their former dwelling.

THE AUTHORITY OF FORBIDDING

The entire spirit world, both angels and demonic entities of all levels, recognize the sonship of Christ—that He is the Son of God. However, when foul and unclean spirits would cry out before departing their victim, identifying Jesus as the Christ (anointed one), Christ forbade them to speak (Luke 4:41; Mark 1:22-25). This was not because these spirits were lying about Christ deity, because Christ is the Son of God. It was because of "guilt by association." To the Pharisees, when demons acknowledged they knew Christ, the Pharisees knew that Satan and demons were liars—so they did not believe what these spirits were saying about Christ being God's son—but they pointed out that the demons knew Christ. In their twisted perception, Christ was in a secret pack with these demons and they were leaving their victims, since Christ worked under the power of a prince spirit controlling all evil spirits name Beelzebub (Matt. 9:34). It would be like a corrupt policeman who is fighting criminals. A criminal is discovered he is to be arrested and brought to trial. The corrupt officer, however, arrests the person but later through outside influence or a bribe, releases the criminal back into society.

Our spiritual authority is provided through the name of Jesus Christ to all believers. This authority must not just be exercised to remove spirits from people; the second half of this authority is to *forbid the spirit from returning*. When Christ encountered the man with at least two thousand spirits, the spirits knew they would be "cast into the pit." This "pit" was referred to in Isaiah 14, when the prophet indicated Lucifer (Satan) would be brought "Down to the sides of the pit." (Isa. 14:12-15). The spirits in the man believed Christ could send them to their final destination, the bottomless pit—called in Greek the Abyss

(Rev. 9:1-11; 17:8; 20:1-3).

When a person is freed though the redemptive covenant, they should verbally speak out and command those spirits to never return to their "house" again. Spiritual authority can lock the door of access when a person refuses to allow cracks in the opening of their house. However, if a person experiencing deliverance chooses to return to their former bondages, they unlock the key to the door and give a huge opening to that spirit to return. When this occurs, the Bible says the last condition of the man is worse than the first.

This explains how when a person having experienced the redemption covenant returns back to their former addictions, their next recovery is often twice as difficult to bring them back to a full deliverance, as a *stronger spirit* often joins with the original spirit of bondage that returns, increasing a "double grip" upon the person. Jesus said it this way:

> *"When an unclean spirit goes out of a man, he goes through dry places seeking rest; and finding none, he says, 'I will return to my house from which I came.' And when he comes, he finds it swept and put in order. Then he goes and takes with him seven other spirit more wicked than himself, and they enter and dwell there; and the last state of that men is worse than the first."*
> —Luke 11:24-26 (NKJV)

I have pondered the question, "What makes one spirit more wicked than others?" The answer as far as "fallen angels" is concerned may be the rank of each angel prior to their rebellion against God, as fallen angels were a part of the one-third that followed Lucifer. Some are principalities (high-level, government-controlling spirits) while others are "powers," spirits with particular power related to sickness and disease, while others control the wickedness in high places.

MY FATHER'S VISION

Many years ago, my father, Fred Stone, was given a troubling vision. I recall him sharing the details with me, and following his death I discovered the handwritten paper in which he recorded the incident. In the vision, he saw me standing facing him, with someone standing on my right and on my left. As he was drawn closer he realized these were not mortal men but were in reality demonic spirits—one being much larger than the other. The larger one was rebuking the smaller one, saying, "Why did you let him get this information on us?" Apparently, the Lord had given me a message or revelation to preach that was troubling to this larger spirit. The smaller one said, "I tried to stop him, and hinder him (speaking of me) but I could not." The stronger, larger spirit then reached into the "belly" of the smaller one and began withdrawing some type of energy or power from him and taking for himself. The smaller one began begging to keep whatever authority or power was being removed from him. It was then that the larger prince spirit made the threat that if the other spirit could not stop me, then he would do so himself.

For years Dad remained in continual intercession for me and petitioned God to restrain the attack of this stronger spirit.

The Scripture recognizes there are different ranks of authority and levels of dominion imparted to spirits. Some are of lesser authority while others are higher up the ladder of supernatural strength and ability. Once possessed, large numbers of spirits can unite in one body, increasing the physical strength of the person. Such was the case when one man was controlled by an estimated two thousand spirits. Out of fear, men in his community attempted to bind him with chains and place him in wooden fetters, and he broke both with little effort.

Spirits that are "wicked" may be a reflection of the level of hatred they have toward God, or the intensity of rebellion they maintain. As an example, there are godly people in the world and many good people in the world; but there are also carnal people, mean people, and evil people, some of whom are far "more wicked" than others. Individuals who exercise more wickedness are possibly under the influence of wicked spirits. One example is the bloodthirsty terrorist organization in Syria and Iraq. Their daily activities including beheading anyone they choose, raping young girls, molesting children, barking out death threats, and stealing money and possessions from innocent people, including seizing their homes. This is just the short list. As if their actions, inspired from their religion of death, is not enough, they boldly and proudly scream

"Allah Akbar" (praise to God) while being drenched in the blood of their beheaded victims. Even those who do not recognize a spirit world often express that some "power" or "unseen force of evil" must be controlling these types of activities.

HOW FAR CAN SATAN GO?

Just how far can Satan go in gaining access into the body, soul, or spirit of a believer? If a believer views Satan as one with unlimited access, unlimited power, and unde-tectable movement, they pen themselves on the mat be-fore the wrestling match begins (Eph. 6:12). Enemies of nations will use false images and misinformation to dis-courage their opponents, even to the point of lying about their strength and military equipment in hopes of gaining a surrender before the war. New territory is always gained after the surrender process. What is worse than losing the battle is to surrender without ever going to battle. Once a believer runs from the roaring lion (Satan—1 Peter 5:8) he will continue to run—not when he *sees* the lion but every time he hears a *roar*.

The answer to "How far can Satan go?" is summed up in one sentence: "As far as a Christian will allow him to go." It is the voice commands and actions of a believer that can shorten or lengthen the rope around the lion's neck. Perhaps you have never heard this said, but the en-tire spirit world is *voice activated*.

God requires faith in your heart and a confession from

your mouth before initiating His act of redemption to-ward you (Rom. 10:10). Christ once saw a blind man cry-ing out to Him and asked the poor fellow, "What would you have me to do?" This was an odd question, since He knew he was blind and knew he wanted healing! However, Christ desired for the man to *ask* for a miracle, since the New Testament spiritual law of receiving from God is to first ask and you shall receive (Matt. 21:22). Christ even reveled that when you have a mountain (a metaphor for a major problem), you must speak to the mountain and command the mountain to be removed. This is because your mountain knows your voice and is activated when you declare the Word of God in pure faith.

Satan and his angels (Rev. 12) are all invisible spirit beings operating in a visible natural world. The entire nat-ural world—all things therein—were originally formed by the Word of God (Heb. 11:3) and are presently still subject to the Word of God. Storms ceased on the Sea of Galilee when Christ spoke, "Peace be still." A living fig tree died within twenty-four hours from the roots up when Christ placed a word curse upon it. Even the irreversible law of gravity that pulls people under water was temporally removed for Peter, when Christ said one word, "Come," and Peter walked on water toward Christ. The first law of thermodynamics says that mass cannot be created or destroyed, just transformed into another form. Yet, Christ took five loaves and two fishes, blessed them with His words, and fed a countless multitude. Wind, rain, trees, mountains, sickness, and demons are all under subjection to the spoken Word of God. When Jesus commanded Satan to get behind Him, there was no argument or legal challenge to Christ's demand. Satan simply "Departed for a season" (Luke 4:13).

Once, when a student at a Christian college asked his professor of theology, "Can a Christian have a demon?" the reply came after a brief pause: "A Christian can 'have' whatever they want to have. "Demonic spirits enter through cracks, through doors, and through various unrepentant sins. Thankfully, the Holy Spirit can assist you in slamming the door on the enemy.

LESSON 6—THE ENEMY ONLY WINS WHEN YOU QUIT FIGHTING

Throughout history a white flag was waved by opposing armies when they knew they were defeated and chose not to be casualties in the remaining fight—they threw up a white flag indicating "surrender." *The enemy wins when we give up.* There is a progression in the process of how faith is lost. First it is lost in the mind, then in the heart, then in the mouth, and finally in the spirit. The mind creates doubt, the heart yields to unbelief, the mouth begins to speak negatively, and eventually the human spirit is defiled. The heart will accept information from the mind, and out of the abundance of the heart the mouth will speak (Luke 6:45).

I have met hundreds of thousands of Christians in my lifetime, and I can recognize when they are considering backing down, backing up, and doing a spiritual U-turn, away from truth. Both their mouth and their actions give them away. When your actions move from obedience to disobedience, and your words from faith to unbelief, and your life from righteous living to carnal pleasure, you become a living target for vexation and oppression.

The rule of engagement for maintaining a protective shield is: "Submit to God and resist the devil and he will flee from you." This is the "S" and "R" factor—submit and resist. Submission means to be obedient and subject to God. In 1 Peter 5:9, the Greek word *anthistemi* means to stand against. Paul wrote in Ephesians about the armor of God and used a known military phrase from his day: "Having done all to stand, stand therefore" (Eph. 6:13-14). The phrase meant that after you have been engaged in a war, and may be weary and exhausted, stand firm and face the enemy knowing you have the ability to defeat the opposition.

THE POWER OF THE CHOICE

All humans living on this planet have been given a free will, meaning the freedom to make their own choices. The power to choose was the option God gave to those who desired to "opt out" of joining His covenant. Of course, those who chose God's laws, statutes, and judgments were given special favors and positive blessings—in their lives, family, possessions, and work—in return for their commitment to God's instruction. "Choose" is used fifty-eight times in fifty-seven verses throughout the Old Testament, at times referring to God selecting Israel as His people from among the nations, and at other times where God instructs Israel to follow Him. Joshua said it this way:

"And if it seems evil to you to serve the Lord, choose for yourselves this day whom you will serve . . ."
—Joshua 24:15 (NKJV)

In the Torah (first five books) the Hebrew word for "choose" is *bachar*, and properly means "to try," "to prove," or "join with." God desired His people to choose the obedience side of their nature and not the rebellious side. A similar Hebrew word is found in Malachi 3:10, where God speaks of Israel bringing their tithes and offerings to the temple. The Almighty instructs His people to "Prove me now . . ." The word *prove* used here is the Hebrew word *bakhan*, and refers to a *test, or to investigate*. It was often used when testing the quality of a precious metal. Choosing God, selecting Him and His instructions, and proving Him in your giving is putting His promise to bless you to a test. It was God who instructed you to place a demand upon him, when He said, "Prove me now . . . saith the Lord."

God gave the title to Israel of His "chosen" (Duet. 7:6; 14:2). Because the root word concealed within *chosen* is linked with *choose,* God the "chooser," who formed Israel as His "son" and His "firstborn" (Exod. 4:22), has authority as a potter does over the clay, to prove, press and test Israel, giving them a righteous path in which to walk with Him. When Israel left Egypt, heading toward a dry, barren and waterless wilderness, God said He would lead Israel through this rugged and lifeless region to "prove them" (Deut. 8:2). The word *prove* used in Deuteronomy 8:2 means "to test," and in many instances it refers to assaying a metal by putting the raw metal, fresh from the ground, into an intense fire, burning out the impurities. Israelites experienced numerous tests in their forty-year journey: needing food and water, being bitten by poisonous snakes, fighting other tribes, and more. When the pressure was applied, the people complained ten times, leading to the collapse of faith among the entire population, with the exception of Joshua and Caleb (Num. 14:24; 38).

Never underestimate the power of making a right or wrong choice. Choices are not just mental decisions. Once released they unleash the power of life and death though your actions taken and your spoken words. We are told that the power of life and death is in the tongue (Prov. 18:21). There are several different Hebrew words translated as "power" throughout the Old Testament. In Proverbs 18:21, the word *power* is *yad* and refers to an open hand. Thus, a person has the power of life and death in their "hand!"

In Israel, there was a family many years ago with five children—four sons and one daughter. Three of the sons were serving in the Israeli military during times of great conflict and two served as fighter pilots. One of the mother's sons, who today is an older man named Boaz, recalls the following incident. Years ago, his mother became so concerned and "stressed out" about her sons and the loss of life in wars that she said to her husband, "I can no longer take the stress of this. I am going to die." The next morning, she was found dead. It was not a suicide and there was no disease in her body. She apparently willed herself to pass on and death came to her house that night!

One of my early friends in Israel was Rabbi Yehudah Getz. He often came to the Western Wall at night, to meet with others, for study and late-night prayers. I had been in his office numerous times and noted his firm dedication to God, for personal prayer and His love for God's Word. He was in good health. However, one day he awoke and told his wife that during the night God spoke to him and told him that he would die in three days. His wife rebuked him, telling him she needed him. He replied to her, "The decision has been made in heaven and I cannot escape God's decision." In three days, he suddenly passed away without any known health issues or physical complications.

In the death of Rabbi Getz, the choice or appointed day was set by God and not the rabbi. In the case of the mother of Boaz, she made a firm decision that she was no longer willing to bear life's burdens, which set in motion the final day of her life. Imagine saying in the morning, "I'm going to die," and the next morning preparations are being made for your funeral. This is certainly an example of the power of death being in the tongue.

This is not to say that we can control the time of our departure by simply saying, "I'm going to heaven now," as "it is appointed unto men once to die . . ." (Heb. 9:27). God does set appointments. However, appointments can be changed or delayed. When King Hezekiah became sick unto death, Isaiah was sent to this King with God's Word to "set his house in order," for he was going to die (2 Kings 20:1). Hezekiah "turned his face toward the wall," which would have been facing the direction of the holy Temple in Jerusalem; the place of the Holy of Holies and the dwelling house of the Ark of the Covenant—God's miniature throne on earth. The sick king wept, crying out for God's mercy. His prayer was so intense, sincere, and effective that before Isaiah could get out of the king's middle courtyard, the voice of God echoed back from the edge of the universe with this message: "I have heard your prayers and seen your tears and will heal you" (1 Kings 20:5). Fifteen more years were added to Hezekiah's (2 Kings 20:6). The appointment with death was altered with intense intercession.

All covenant promises in the New Testament must be believed or chosen for yourself. The Bible tells us that Christ came to give us life and give it more abundantly (John 10:10). The Greek word translated here as abundantly is *perissos* and means "superabundant" in quantity and quality. Let me explain. Eternal life is a free gift, but abundant life is a choice. Eternal life is God's gift to you, but abundant life is your gift back to God. Eternal life is in the future, but abundant life is now. Eternal life abides in you, but abundant life is all around you. Your abundant life in always linked to your purpose in life. When people live without a purpose they are always making wrong choices, connecting with wrong people, and living with the results of their actions.

Never give up in the night what God gives you in the light.

Summary

In reviewing this entire book, I pondered over some final thoughts I could leave with you, the reader, that would serve as brief nuggets in summing up what I would like to drop in your spirit for further assistance. Here they are:

God and Satan are Not Co-equal

God and Satan never have been, nor ever will be co-equal. The reason Satan is perceived, at times, to have more "power," is that his operational strategies impact the world of idols, pagans, false religions, and evil governments; thus, his influence is all around us. Because evil is global, the perception is that Satan is in dominant control. In reality, God's final plan will trump the goals of Satan's dark kingdom and in the end God wins—for eternity!

I Will – I Won't

The human will can either be your greatest blessing or worse curse, depending upon how it's power is activated. Your will power not only controls your choices and actions, but your self-control and resistance strength. When the human will becomes submitted to God and His Word, choosing to follow His precepts, then the seeds of blessing are planted for a future harvest. However, if your will focuses on rebellion, stubbornness, or resisting God's Word, then any blessings cease. Use your will wisely.

EXALT GOD'S ABILITY AND NOT SATAN'S ABILITY

Throughout my ministry, when I see some Christians in a spiritual battle, they often center on the conflict and not the resolution. When a ministry problem is presented to me, I refuse to play in the blame game but immediately seek a solution. God can do the impossible (Luke 1:37), therefore there is nothing Satan can send that God's postal service cannot stamp on the package, "Return to Sender."

YOU ARE NOT AN ORPHAN—YOU HAVE A FATHER AND A FAMILY

A person in covenant with Christ must understand they are not fatherless, as an orphan, but have a true Heavenly Father. Jesus said He would not leave us comfortless (John 14:18). The Greek word for comfortless is *orphanos*, alluding to being parentless. The Holy Spirit is our comforter (John 14:16). The Greek word is *paraklotos*, meaning "one who comes along side of to assist." During all spiritual warfare, we are not alone but have supernatural assistance at all times. The family of God consists of followers of

Christ from around the world, and every person in covenant with Christ has a family!

AUTHORITY IS LEGAL NOT JUST MENTAL

By this I mean our authority is not mental ascent, in which we mentally convince ourselves of something, hoping that by mentally agreeing, it will bring it to pass. Christ presented to His followers His name, His blood, and His word which in the realm of spirits gives us legal authority over all the authority of Satan, in the same manner that a judge's decision in court is legal and final. You don't just believe your way into victory, you believe, confess and act on Christ's finished work.

CHRIST'S VICTORY OVER SATAN IS COMPLETE

This is a major point. Christ has totally defeated Satan, death, hell, and the grave. Every spiritual struggle has already been given a solution revealed somewhere in the Word of God. For some it is fasting, for others intense prayer, for some it is discipline of the mind, body, and spirit. For some it is rebuking and resisting temptation. Inaction and indecision leads to defeat. All the enemy must do to win is get us to do nothing.

You Will Never Have a Test that Someone Has Not Already Passed

At times when an intense test, temptation or trial strikes us, we feel alone as though no one has ever gone through what we are going through. Yet, Paul wrote that there is "no temptation taken you but that such is common to man" (1 Cor. 10:13). The Bible tells us, "For in that He Himself has suffered, being tempted, he is able to aid those who are tempted." (Heb. 2:18 NKJV). Jesus was tested in "all points" and passed the test. Jesus passed the test. Somewhere there is someone who has already passed the test that you are going through, providing you can also pass through.

You Control the Door

A door is an opening into your home or your personal life. Christ told the church He was standing on the outside knocking to get in (Rev. 3:20). If Christ is not in your fellowship it's because you never let Him in! If any type of evil or unclean spirit is not in your life, it is also because you have not let him in, as you control the door to your heart, the door of you mind, and the door of your spirit. You can allow or refuse anyone who knocks on those doors.

All Spirits are Subject to Christ

The authority of Jesus Christ is known globally throughout the spirit world. Missionaries have demonstrated the authority in the name of Jesus, in every nation where the Gospel has been preached. When speaking His name, a person must have "faith in the name" (Acts 3:16) and just casually, without unction, speak His name.

FEEDING DEMONS

Just as angels eat manna (see Exod. 16:35) which is called "angel's food" (Psa. 78:25), demon spirits are "fed" by the levels of sin they can create through influence, control, or possession. In Genesis, God said that the serpent would crawl and would eat dust from the earth. It is interesting that man was created from dust and at death the flesh decays and returns to dust (Gen. 2:7, 3:19). The serpent, a symbol of Satan thrives in the dust of the ground. Because dirt and flesh are linked the works of the flesh feed the sin nature in men, and demonic spirits thrive in the mind and spirit of those who practice and enjoy sin. Saying it another way, demons can thrive and "feed" off the flesh or carnal nature in men.

To close the doors, believers must feed their souls and spirits those things that pertain until life and not the desires of the lust of the flesh, lust of the eyes, and pride of life (1 John 2:16).